NEW JERSEY BREWERIES

NEW JERSEY BREWERIES

LEW BRYSON & MARK HAYNIE

STACKPOLE
BOOKS

Published by
STACKPOLE BOOKS
5067 Ritter Road
Mechanicsburg, PA 17055
www.stackpolebooks.com

The authors and publisher encourage readers to visit the breweries and sample their beers and recommend that those who consume alcoholic beverages travel with a nondrinking driver.

Printed in the United States of America

10 9 8 7 6 5 4 3 2 1

FIRST EDITION

Cover design by Caroline Stover

Labels and logos are used with permissions from the breweries

Library of Congress Cataloging-in-Publication Data

Bryson, Lew.
   New Jersey breweries / Lew Bryson & Mark Haynie.
      p.   cm.
   Includes index.
   ISBN-13: 978-0-8117-3504-9 (pbk.)
   ISBN-10: 0-8117-3504-4 (pbk.)
   1. Bars (Drinking establishments)—New Jersey—Guidebooks. 2. Breweries—New Jersey—Guidebooks. 3. Microbreweries—New Jersey—Guidebooks. 4. Beer—New Jersey—Guidebooks. I. Haynie, Mark, 1950– II. Title.
TX950.57.N5B79   2008
647.95749—dc22
                                                      2007052800

To my children Thomas and Nora
Unreservedly the best kids I know

LB

To my wife Mary Lu
Who has been the rock on which I lean

MH

CONTENTS

ACKNOWLEDGMENTS

Whew. This was a rush. Mark and I undertook this book on a short schedule, figuring we could easily swing it, with only twenty breweries and a relatively small area to cover. Let me tell you: New Jersey's small, but it's action-packed.

First, thanks go to my partner, Mark Haynie. Mark did a lot of the brewery legwork on this book, and he took my criticisms and suggestions on his writing with his customary endearing cheerfulness. He taught me a few things about enthusiasm and adaptability too. Nice work, Mark; I could not have done this one without you.

Thanks again to Kyle Weaver, my editor at Stackpole, who asked me for two years, "How about that New Jersey book?" Points for persistence, Kyle, and patience too.

I'd also like to thank those intrepid folks who keep the torch of beer appreciation burning: the bar owners, retailers, and specialty wholesalers. Supporting beer variety in New Jersey has been a tough haul, but you folks are up to the job.

My gratitude as well to the folks who helped us find the best in the Garden State. That's the users who keep things up-to-date on two first-class beer websites: BeerAdvocate.com and Pubcrawler.com. Thanks for some excellent tips; I wouldn't have found Tierney's without you. Two very good friends of mine in New Jersey, Mike Gates and Rich Pawlak, have dragged me around to some top-notch places for food and beer; that was a great night at the Jug Handle, guys.

Special thanks to Bruce Springsteen, Southside Johnny, and John Gorka, who filled my car with appropriate tunes as I cruised around the state, trying not to get lost "somewhere in the swamps of Jersey."

My father, Lew, gave me unfailing map support, as usual. My children, Thomas and Nora, take everything in stride—latchkey afternoons, late dinners, bottles and growlers all over the house—and always welcome me home. And as ever, my wife, Catherine, made it all possible. I can never thank her enough.

To all of you, cheers!

LB

"What a long strange trip it's been," to use a hackneyed quote. The road to this point has been filled with good beers, good friends, and lots of interesting places. I would first like to acknowledge my friend and coauthor, Lew Bryson, who had the faith to include me in this project and whose words of encouragement got me through it. It was a great learning experience, as well as a lot of fun.

Then there are those without whom this book would not exist: the brewers and owners of the breweries and brewpubs of New Jersey. They are not a large group, but a dedicated one. They have resolved to make the best beers available despite having to deal with arcane laws and a restrictive system. Thank you from the bottom of my glass!

I'd also like to mention my good friend and colleague Gary Monterosso, who got me started writing about beer and introduced me to so many people over the years. He helped me spread my wings and fly. I would be remiss not to mention my other friends and colleagues at the New Jersey Association of Beerwriters, Kurt Epps, Kevin Trayner, and Jim Carlucci, who have helped me on my journey.

No beer dedication would be complete without a doff of the hat to the late Michael Jackson, who made the beer world what it is today and blazed trails for beerwriters and beer lovers worldwide. Our many travels with the Beerhunter will always be the highlight of my beer experience. The world seems a little less interesting without him.

Also, my favorite "old curmudgeon," Jack Curtin, and "Joe Six-pack" Don Russell deserve praise. Along with Lew, they are my inspirations. I wish I could see the world through their glasses and put it to paper like they do. Keep up the good work, guys.

I'm grateful to my friends Tom Baker and Peggy Zwerver, late of Heavyweight Brewing, who allowed me to become part of their "family" and learn what it takes to run a brewery. We enjoyed the trips, the fests, the parties, even all the work. May those days come again!

I'd also like to express my appreciation to Tony Forder of *Ale Street News*, who has given me a chance to prove myself. His work on bringing beer culture to the New Jersey–New York metro area is legendary. Keep the faith, Tony!

Then there's my father, who discovered Belgian beers back during World War II and I guess passed it on genetically. My father was not a big beer drinker, but I can recall tasting those Ballantine XXXs when I was a boy. Funny what you remember.

Finally, thanks to my wife, Mary Lu, without whom traveling would not be as much fun. She loves to beer travel as much as I do, and we have put a lot of miles into searching for the best brews. Being a beer lover too, she understands when I have to buy that special beer or want to travel 100 miles for a beer dinner. I couldn't have done it without her support.

MH

INTRODUCTION

Welcome to *New Jersey Breweries!* It's about time, too. After writing all around it with other brewery guides, and joking about *New Jersey Breweries, a Pamphlet*, I finally admitted I needed help with this incredibly complex state. New Jersey's the most densely populated state, and its breweries live up to that, packing many kinds of beer and business models into their ranks. That I could handle. But when it came to actually making sense of it in terms of explaining the state, I had to get a native.

Mark Haynie grew up in the Atlantic City area, and has lived there all his life. His experience and insights on New Jersey, coupled with a love of beer that has led him to log thousands of miles traveling to visit new breweries, made him the perfect partner. Together we tackled this state and its beermakers and tried to make sense of it.

New Jersey is a study in contrasts. Like the state itself, which encompasses both the jam-packed suburbs and intensely commercial and industrial zones along the Hudson River in the north; the flat, quiet, and undeveloped reaches of the Pine Barrens in the middle; and the ridged and rolling open space of the Skylands in the northwest, brewing in New Jersey presents some odd juxtapositions. There's the massive Anheuser-Busch plant outside Newark, surrounded by brewpubs scattered through every kind of town setting. Small breweries are obviously a success in New Jersey, with well over half of them more than ten years old, but only one new brewpub has opened in the past five years.

Perhaps the most confusing contrast is the one between the success of New Jersey's small brewers and the continuing lack of a solid and pervasive "beer culture" in the state, the stubborn nonappearance of the niche for beer-focused bars that is thriving just over the border in Pennsylvania and New York. Part of it is New Jersey's very population density: population-based bar licenses make it incredibly expensive to open a bar, with licenses going for as much as $2 million in the Cherry Hill area. But it's not cheap to open a bar in New York City either, and there are more beer-focused bars and high-end taps in Manhattan and Brooklyn than there are in New Jersey.

Beer lovers in the area routinely refer to South Jersey as the "Beer Wasteland." Beer bar owners in Philly joke about having to spend September recalibrating customers' palates after they've spent August "down the shore" drinking mainstream beer. The few New Jersey bars that truly focus on providing a variety of beer and the brewpubs that have proven themselves are gratefully embraced.

Why is New Jersey behind the curve? Frankly, we don't know. Because all the pieces are—and have been—in place: good breweries making a variety of beer; an active beer press in the form of fifteen-year-old *Ale Street News*, published right here in New Jersey; and enthusiasts who pushed things, such as Ed Busch, who was instrumental in getting the state's brewpub law passed, the late Richie Stolarz, a tireless organizer of beer tastings and dinners who never missed an opportunity to talk good beer, and the great Chris Demetri, also sadly missed, who had made the Old Bay in New Brunswick into one of the premiere beer bars on the East Coast in the mid-1990s.

It is our sincere hope that the book you hold in your hands will help. Take it and go beer traveling; loan it to your friends (better yet, buy them their own copies!); most of all, read it and realize that as good as New Jersey's beer scene is, *it could be better*. It would be great if some of the restrictive laws on brewpub and small brewery sales could be changed. It would be marvelous if people—drinkers, bar managers, restaurant owners—were more open to variety. It would be truly wonderful if the next edition of *New Jersey Breweries* were twice as thick because of a boom in new breweries and beer bars.

It's in your hands. We've done what we could—and enjoyed it! Now it's up to you. You have your mission: Support New Jersey beer. Get out there and give it your best; the brewers have done nothing less for you.

American Brewing, New Jersey Brewing

The ships that made their way from the ports of Europe to colonize the New World were filled with people who were willing to undergo great hardships for the possibility of a better life. Provisions to keep these people nourished on the long voyage were oftentimes found to be sorely lacking, particularly their beer.

Beer was an important asset onboard, as it was used to prevent scurvy. Many times, the crews aboard the ships hijacked much of it so that they would have enough for the return trip, leaving the colonists with little to no rations. This predicament forced the Puritans to land in Plymouth instead of farther south as planned. Though the people heartily mistrusted water as a beverage, they found that the water in the New World was drinkable, unlike at home. Beer was still the drink of choice, however, and they needed to find ways to brew this beverage in their new home.

In the early colonies, as back in England, the women shouldered the duties of brewing for the family, mostly table beer, but as the colonies grew, production breweries sprouted up in a multitude of places for the commercial sale of their "universal beverage." Malt and beer were primarily shipped from Great Britain, but not in quantities enough to satisfy the needs of the colonists. Most of the time, the beer was not the best once it reached the shores of the New World anyway.

Barley became a sought-after crop, and most of the colonies attempted to cultivate it, some with little success. They therefore depended on supplies from other settlements. New Jersey, with its rich, fertile farmland, became a leading supplier of the grain for the region. But the demand outweighed the supply, so the colonists needed to adapt and use other products that were fermentable. They found that corn made a nice brew, but it did not attain popularity in many places. Molasses, sugar, pumpkins, apples, even persimmons were brewed into various alcoholic libations. As a matter of fact, the ciders of New Jersey were considered the best in the world at this time and were shipped throughout the colonies.

Surrounded by the major brewing cities of New York and Philadelphia, New Jersey did not have a critical need for breweries, though many small facilities were established in the larger settlements to produce alcoholic beverages for consumption in their area as well as some for export.

Breweries popped up all over the state. In 1641, one of the first commercial breweries in New Jersey was started by Aert Tewnissen Van Patten, who leased property in Hoboken to start a farm and a brewery. Despite all his hard work, the Indians decided they weren't happy with him there and destroyed all but the brewhouse in 1643. Thus ended the first attempt at establishing a brewery in the state. No one else was willing to attempt it at this location. Late in the 1600s, the Salem colony in southwestern New Jersey was home to several breweries in Elsinboro Township. Names such as Thompson's, Nicholson's, Morris's, and Abbot's were known throughout the area.

Burlington, New Brunswick, Trenton, Elizabeth, Mount Holly, Lamberton, Newark, Hackettstown, Weehawken, and Hoboken all had several breweries operating at one time or another. All of these cities had one thing in common—location. They had access to either a river or one of the main roads that connected the larger settlements.

Burlington, a thriving port on the Delaware River close to Philadelphia, became a center of trade. From here, finished products such as beer, bread, beef, and pork were shipped to the Caribbean islands of Barbados and Jamaica. From the late seventeenth century until well into the nineteenth century, breweries opened and closed in the city, supplying ports they serviced with their fine brews.

New Brunswick took advantage of its location near the mouth of the Raritan and its proximity to New York via the King's Highway to become another hub of brewing. At least eight breweries have existed in this town since its inception in 1730.

Wheels were set in motion in 1805 that would make history in the annals of brewing, not only in New Jersey, but nationwide. Gen. John N. Cumming founded the Newark Brewery and sold draft and bottled porter and double and single ale. The brewery was purchased in 1832 by Robert Morton, who kept the kettles producing until 1838, when it was leased by Thain and Collins.

In 1840, Peter Ballantine moved from Albany, New York, to Newark and leased the brewery, opening the Patterson and Ballantine Brewing Company. He soon bought out his partner and changed the name to P. Ballantine and Sons. Under him and his sons, Peter Jr., John H., and Robert F., the Newark brewery flourished. New facilities covering 12 acres of land were built on the Passaic River to accommodate lager brewing in 1879. By the end of the century, this was the sixth-largest brewery in the United States. When the final son died in 1905, the company passed to George Griswold Frelinghuysen, who was married to Peter's granddaughter.

The company was acquired in 1933 by Carl and Otto Badenhausen, who grew the brewery through shrewd advertising to the number-three spot in the country. The forties and fifties were good times for the Ballantine brand, but the sixties saw a decline in sales, and in 1971, Falstaff bought up Ballantine and closed the brewery for good. Production moved to the Narragansett plant in Rhode Island, which Falstaff had acquired in 1965. Pabst purchased Falstaff in 1975, and the Ballantine products moved yet again, this time to Indiana, and have been moving ever since.

Thus a long and glorious history of one of the greatest brands to come out of the Garden State came to a sad and tragic end. Its beers are still remembered with reverence today, and unopened bottles are sold and traded on the Internet. The India Pale Ale was legendary, as it was aged in wood for one year prior to bottling. The brewers would then select the best batches to be aged for ten years or more before bottling it as the legendary Ballantine Burton Ale. The Burton Ale was never sold; it was given to company executives, distributors, and celebrities as personalized Christmas gifts.

Ballantine's three-ring sign was known worldwide; "Purity, Body & Flavor" were the watchwords of the brand. The products available today are but a pale version of what they once were. I can remember, as a youngster, my father allowing me to taste his Ballantine XXX. I thought it was rather bitter then, but the memories of that beer have stuck with me my whole life.

Newark continued to be a big player in the New Jersey brewing scene, with a large number of smaller breweries opening and closing throughout the nineteenth and twentieth centuries—names like Hill and Krueger, Peter Hauck and Company, Fehleisen and Company, Union Brewing Company, Eagle Brewing Company, Essex County Brewing Company, George W. Wiedenmayer, and the one remaining brewery in the area, Anheuser-Busch. In its heyday, Newark was home to more than twenty-five breweries at one time.

Once again a brewery from New Jersey made history when, in 1935, Gottfried Krueger Brewing Company was the first to package its beer in cans. An agreement with American Can Company in 1933 led to a major revolution in the way beer was marketed and retailed. Within a year or two, all the major players jumped on the canwagon, and even though this innovation has gone through major technological changes over the years, it is still a large part of the market today.

By the dawn of the twentieth century, there were fifty-one breweries in the state, producing a total of almost 2.5 million barrels of beer per annum. This placed New Jersey about seventh in the nation for beer production. But by this time, the farming of barley in the Garden State was practically nonexistent, and only one malting house remained.

World War I had a profound effect on breweries everywhere. Mistrust of the immigrant German beer barons found the public looking at alternatives to the fine lagers produced by their companies. Then there were shortages of metals and agricultural products used to make weapons and provide food for the soldiers overseas. The patriotic fervor fueled the argument of the various antialcohol organizations that the United States become a dry country.

Prohibition, the "Noble Experiment," which passed in 1919 and took effect in 1920, saw the brewing industry suffer the biggest shakeout in history. Those who could not survive by making "near beer," soda, malt syrup, ice cream, or some other product shut their doors forever, many losing everything they had invested.

When alcohol became legal again in 1933, only a few of the larger breweries were prepared to resume production. In the next year, a plethora of small breweries attempted to make a go of it. But they could not compete with the technologically superior brewers who had honed their craft during the shutdown. Those who had continued in the drinks sector during the years of Prohibition and had kept up with new technology in bottling lines were ready for the "take-home" generation. With widespread use of refrigerators in homes, and after thirteen years of not having a local tavern to drink in, workers now wanted to take their beer home with them, and draft beer had lost much of its market. By the end of 1934, there were approximately 756 breweries remaining in the United States, less than 25 of those in the entire state of New Jersey.

Just as the economy was heading into an upturn, world politics once again brought a possible menace to the brewing industry. World War II was not a totally unexpected event, and brewers tried to minimize the effect of the wartime shortages on their production. The beer can was the first casualty, as tin was needed elsewhere. Bottles were in good supply, but crowns were not. Recycling of caps and use of larger bottles reduced the necessity for the item, thus averting a possible disaster. Overall, the demand for beer actually rose during the war years. Memories of Prohibition still haunted the country, and that mistake was not repeated, though not for lack of trying by the drys.

New Jersey seems to have weathered this period fairly well, losing only a few facilities to the economy. Several also changed hands or consolidated.

After the war, national breweries jockeyed for position, and the consolidation trend hit a fever pitch. In order to compete on a national level, owning multiple locations became a necessity to be able to supply the needed quantities of beer, and this also facilitated the distribution process.

In the mid-1940s, brewing giant Anheuser-Busch of St. Louis, Missouri, purchased 50 acres of prime property in Newark. This was a big step for the St. Louis brewery, but a necessary one. Later in the decade, the company began to construct its most modern and largest brewery to date. In 1951, this behemoth brewery began production, and in 1954, A-B followed up with the opening of a Los Angeles facility, soon cementing its first-place status in the brewery wars.

In 1961, the Gottfried Krueger Brewing Company of Newark was absorbed by the Narragansett Brewing Company of Cranston, Rhode Island, in a five-year lease. The Krueger brand would be distributed from the Rhode Island plant, and Narragansett would be distributed in New York City from Newark. This lease never finished its course, as Falstaff bought Narragansett in 1965 and closed the Newark plant to produce all the brands in Rhode Island. An antitrust lawsuit brought against the company by the government led to its demise and subsequent acquisition by Pabst. Since then, all of these brands eventually disappeared from the market and are just a memory to their aficionados.

What started as the Trenton Brewing Company in 1892 became Peoples Brewing in 1899. It was ultimately bought by Metropolis Brewing in 1950, becoming a contender along with its other subsidiaries throughout the East Coast.

P. Ballantine and Sons was one of the last remaining bastions of a single-site brewery, but we've already seen what consequences that produced.

The Orange Brewing Company, established in 1901, brewed until Prohibition and sold out in 1934 to John F. Trommer Inc. and then to Liebmann Breweries of Brooklyn in 1950. Liebmann was the bottler of Rheingold Extra Dry of the "Miss Rheingold" fame. This eventually became the sole location where Rheingold was produced. In 1977, it was shuttered, and Rheingold was no more until reincarnated in 1999 by another of the Liebmann family. It experienced limited nostalgic success and was purchased by Drinks America in 2005.

Now there is but one remaining vestige of that golden era of brewing—Anheuser-Busch in Newark. It is certainly the largest brewery in New Jersey, with production of more than 7 million barrels a year.

Small Brewing Returns to New Jersey
The era of the microbrewery and brewpub started in the early 1990s, and several players have stepped up to keep up the long tradition of quality brewing in the Garden State. Climax Brewing of Roselle Park opened in 1994 and began the craft-brewing revolution in the state. Dave Hoffmann, with his father, Kurt, as his assistant, brews some of the finest English and German classic styles around. Flying Fish Brewing Company of Cherry Hill began as a virtual brewery on the Web while its owner, Gene Muller, got all his fish in a row. In 1996, the beer began flowing from his tanks, and his business has since taken wing. His is now the largest craft brewery in the state and still growing. River Horse Brewing in Lambertville began to brew in the same year and has been another success story. This brewery was recently acquired by several Philadelphia investors, and bigger and better things are planned.

When the trend for the smaller breweries became popular, a multitude of them opened or attempted to open, but others never got off the planning table. Names like Blue Collar Brewing of Vineland, Hoboken Brewing, and the Red Bank Brewery all have been written into the

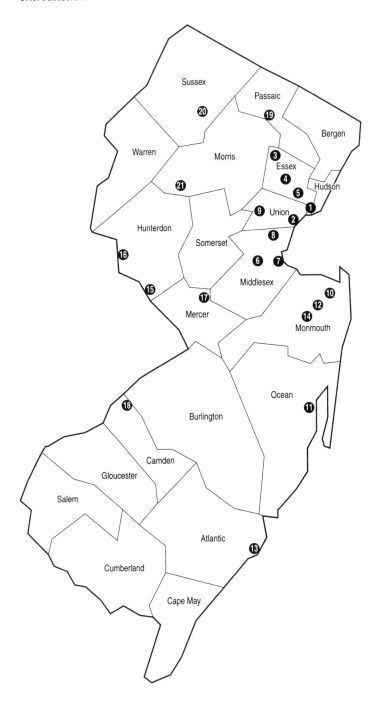

1. Anheuser-Busch, Newark
2. Climax Brewing, Roselle Park
3. Cricket Hill Brewing Company, Fairfield
4. Egan and Sons, Montclair
5. Gaslight Brewery and Restaurant, South Orange
6. Harvest Moon Brewery, New Brunswick
7. J. J. Bitting Brewing Company, Woodbridge
8. Pizzeria Uno, Metuchen
9. Trap Rock Restaurant and Brewery, Berkeley Heights
10. The Original Basil T's Brewery and Italian Grill, Red Bank
11. Basil T's Brewpub and Italian Grill, Toms River
12. Laird and Company, Scobeyville
13. Tun Tavern, Atlantic City
14. Brewer's Apprentice, Freehold
15. River Horse Brewing Company, Lambertville
16. The Ship Inn, Milford
17. Triumph Brewing Company, Princeton
18. Flying Fish Brewing Company, Cherry Hill
19. High Point Brewing Company, Butler
20. Krogh's Restaurant and Brew Pub, Sparta
21. Long Valley Pub and Brewery, Long Valley

pages of history. No story about New Jersey brewing would be complete without a mention of Heavyweight Brewing of Ocean Township. Tom Baker and Peg Zwerver opened up in 1999 to immediate accolades for their distinct and bold beers. They put New Jersey back on the beer map around the world. Though Heavyweight was a success, they decided to shut down and look at other options in the brewing and restaurant business. Another page turned.

In 1994, a law allowing brewpubs passed, and several brewers didn't waste time getting them operational. The Ship Inn in Milford was the first to open, in January 1995. Triumph in Princeton was soon to follow, two months later, and Long Valley Pub and Brewery in October. Harvest Moon and Basil T's Red Bank began operations in 1996; J. J. Bitting, Basil T's Toms River, and Trap Rock in 1997; and Tun Tavern, Pizzeria Uno, and Gaslight in 1998. Krogh's added a brewery in 1999.

Several brewpubs opened between 1995 and 1997 but have either ceased brewing or closed. The Mill Hill Saloon in Trenton and the Stone Tavern in Bernardsville continue on as bars, and Mill Hill still has a good selection of taps, but Jersey Jim's in Hillsborough, Kokomo's in Wildwood, Joshua Huddy's in Toms River, and Cedar Creek in Egg Harbor City are just ghosts on the Internet, memories of beers past . . . some good, some not so.

New Jersey has been and still is home to some of the best beer in the nation. We're sure that this tradition will be carried on for many years to come.

Bibliography

Baron, Stanley. *Brewed in America: A History of Beer and Ale in the United States.* Boston: Little, Brown, 1962.

Van Wieren, Dale P. *American Breweries II.* West Point, PA: East Coast Breweriana Association, 1995.

Weiss, Harry B., and Grace M. Weiss. *Early Breweries in New Jersey.* Trenton: NJ Agricultural Society, 1963.

100 Years of Brewing. New York: Arno Press, 1903.

How to Use This Book

This book is a compendium of information about New Jersey's breweries. It also lists some of the interesting attractions and best bars in New Jersey. And it offers facts and opinions about brewing, brewing history in the United States and New Jersey, and beer-related subjects.

It does not present a comprehensive history of any brewery, nor is it a book that tries to rate every single beer produced by every single brewery. It is not a conglomeration of beer jargon—Original Gravities, International Bittering Unit levels, Apparent Attenuations, and so on. And it's not about homebrewing. Other people have done a fine job on books like that, but it's not what we wanted to do.

It is a travel guide about breweries and New Jersey, a state blessed with great natural beauty—long beaches and barrier islands, the deep forests of the Pine Barrens, the long rolling ridges in the north—and with a friendly, industrious populace that finds comfort and leisure in a suburbia that sprawls like no other. Sharing information has been a central part of the success of the rise of microbreweries in the United States. We've been sharing what we know for a combined span of almost forty years, and this book and its companion volumes: *Pennsylvania Breweries; New York Breweries;* and *Virginia, Maryland, and Delaware Breweries,* represent our efforts to spread the good word.

The book is organized in alternating parts. The meat of the book, the brewery information, is presented in five sections. The first section covers the industrial heartland of New Jersey and the huge brewery that produces clean, crisp beer in the midst of it, Anheuser-Busch. Each of the four geographic sections—the New York suburbs, the shore, the west, and the north—is prefaced with a description of the area for those unfamiliar with it. The "A word about . . ." sections are intended as instructional interludes on topics you may be curious about. There should be something there for almost everyone, whether novice, dabbler, or fanatic.

The history and character, highlights, personal observations, and other information about the brewpub or brewery are presented in a narrative section. A brewpub sells beer to be enjoyed on location, whereas a brewery sells its beer primarily off-premises. If any beers have won Great American Beer Festival (GABF) awards, those are noted, but not every brewery enters these competitions. The annual capacity in barrels, as listed for each brewery, is a function of the fermenting-tank capacity and the average time to mature a beer. Lagers take longer, so on two identical systems with the same fermenter setup, an all-lager brewery would have significantly lower annual capacity than an all-ale brewery.

The other area beer sites listed for most breweries may include multitaps, historic bars, or restaurants with good beer selections. Whenever possible, we visited these bars and had at least one beer there. Inevitably, though, a few of these descriptions are based on recommendations from brewers or beer geeks we know personally.

We urge you not to get too caught up in trying to guess which one of us wrote a particular entry. This was a team effort, and we feel the outcome is our book, not Mark's book or Lew's book. We hope you enjoy reading it, and we hope it gets you out on the road, looking for the next exit for good beer.

The Big Red One

A nheuser-Busch stands alone, at least in New Jersey. It is by far the biggest brewery in the state. It's also the only brewery right in the heart of the industrial plain that spreads west from the Hudson, split by the New Jersey Turnpike. Drive by on the Turnpike or ride the Amtrak train, and you'll see what looks like just another big factory building, maybe more steam coming out of it than most. But if it's nighttime, you'll see the red glow of the big neon sign on top of the brewery, a flying representation of the Anheuser-Busch eagle. Yes, it says, we're here, in New Jersey, beside the refineries, beside the Newark Airport, beside the docks and marshes, and we make Budweiser beer.

Do you wonder where they get their water, out there in the middle of what looks like a landscape from the last desperate moments of *The Lord of the Rings?* I sure did, so I asked. "We get our water from the same place people around here get their drinking water," answers Scott Mennen, the senior resident brewmaster at Newark. That's from reservoirs upstate, near Pompton Lakes. "Then we take it through filtering and other things here in the brewery to get it exactly the way we want it."

He chuckled darkly. "New Jersey gets a bad rap."

I'm sure he empathizes, because sometimes, so does Anheuser-Busch (A-B). Some of you are probably wondering why we put this huge brewery in a book about microbreweries and brewpubs. This is not just a book about small breweries, it's about *New Jersey* breweries, and as A-B is the state's largest, we could hardly leave it out. A-B is the world's second-largest brewer, with approximately 48 percent of the U.S. market and 8 percent of the world's market. The brewery in Newark is only one of their twelve breweries in the United States, a diversified production plan that allows A-B to deliver beer across the country, as fresh as possible. The Newark brewery also provides excellent jobs for New Jersey residents.

But there's another reason they're in here: The truth needs to be told about Anheuser-Busch.

The truth? Yes, truth, because there's a lot of silliness out there. Because Bud Light is the best-selling beer in America, A-B is often the whipping boy of the microbrewers. A-B has taken its share of shots at the micros as well, to be sure; that's business.

The truth is, A-B has more than a hundred highly trained and qualified brewmasters who are fanatical about quality in ingredients and process. I've met some of them. They're nice guys, but just between you and me, they're nuts. One of them talked to me for an hour about their yeast; it was as if he couldn't stop himself. Because A-B is so huge and so profitable, they can afford to do their own research on barley strains (they have a barley research institute), and malting (they have three of their own maltings), and hops (they have several hops farms), and rice (they have two rice mills), and yeast (they have . . . well, you get the picture).

Why so much research, why so much fanaticism? Trace it back to the true founder of the business, Adolphus Busch. After marrying Bavarian Brewery owner Eberhard Anheuser's daughter, Adolphus bought into the business in 1865. He took it from a penny-ante operation to a strong regional brewery. Part of the reason for this success was his superb salesmanship abilities. Adolphus was reputed to use every trick in the book, and some unpublished ones to boot.

But another large component was his obsession with quality. Adolphus traveled widely in Europe and America, sampling beers, studying brewing processes, and evaluating malts and hops. He wrote long letters with detailed instructions on purchasing the finest malt and how to best use it to make excellent beer. "You cannot make a fine beer with inferior malt," he said in one letter I've seen.

This obsession continues today. A-B buys only the finest hops they can find; I've talked to independent hops brokers who confirm it. Their maltings are top-notch operations. They buy the best equipment and maintain it perfectly, and they have a solid commitment to environmental stewardship.

That's why I laugh when earnest beer geeks say, "If Anheuser-Busch wanted to, with their talent and equipment and quality control, they could make the best beer in the world." As far as A-B is concerned, they already do make the best beer in the world. It's called Budweiser.

Come along and we'll take a look at how it's done.

Anheuser-Busch

200 U.S. Highway 1, Newark, NJ 07114
www.budweiser.com; www.anheuser-busch.com

Technically, this isn't the right kind of thing for a guidebook to do. The Newark Anheuser-Busch brewery doesn't offer tours, and you can't visit this place, so this is a guide to something you can't go to. But I've been through three of the company's breweries, and I can try to give you a feel for what's going on. Here's what I saw at the Baldwinsville, New York, facility that impressed me. Newark's pretty much the same, with some minor differences.

The brewery is enormous. The four big brewkettles (Newark has five), the massive mash tuns, the aerators (an Anheuser-Busch innovation in which the wort trickles down against blasts of warm air to remove sulfites), and the chip tanks are all controlled from a slickly automated command center. I walked all over the brewery, from the rail siding where six to eight railcars of malt come in every day, to the brewhouse where about twenty-three batches of beer are made every day, to the packaging hall where almost 270,000 cases of beer are bottled every day, to the loading dock where better than two hundred semi-trailer truckloads of beer go out every day. I was blown away by the size.

The chip tanks are the lagering tanks where the famous beechwood aging takes place. I've seen it; I've held the beechwood. Thin strips of beechwood, about 18 inches long and 1.5 inches wide, are boiled numerous times, then spread in the bottom of the chip tanks by hand. They provide a settling place for the yeast in the beer. The chips are used three times, then dumped.

This is "beechwood aging"? The theory is that without the chips, the yeast would be crushed by the weight of the beer. A-B brewers have told me that they've done batches without the beechwood, and they could taste the difference. I believe them, because this *has* to be an expensive process, with lots of labor involved in handling the chips, plus the purchase and process of the chips themselves. (They come from Tennessee and south

Beers brewed: Budweiser, Bud Light, Busch, Busch Light, Natural Light, Natural Ice, King Cobra, Michelob Ultra, Rolling Rock, and Rock Green Light, all year-round beers.

Missouri, by the way.) A-B wouldn't do something that expensive if there weren't a good reason.

The chip tanks are huge, with specialized equipment you won't find anywhere else. They're expensive and exacting, all in the service of consistency of product. This is the heart of A-B's story and of their success. They do things their way, they are unafraid to spend on fanatical stretches of quality, and they plan for the future. I have a lot of respect for that.

The Pick: I really do think the Rolling Rock out of Newark tastes like the original, and Scott and his associates and bosses have gone to great lengths to make it so. If you can't bring yourself to drink it for sentimental reasons, I understand; go on out and look for the freshest Born-On Bud you can find.

I did get a chance to talk to Scott Mennen, the senior resident brewmaster at Newark. He's been with A-B since 1987, when he was a newly graduated engineer. "Part of it's a process, part of it's an art," he said, explaining why he was drawn to brewing. "A lot of it's engineering. You're dealing with raw materials, heat transfer. But to understand beer, you have to learn the art." He learned the art and has been the head brewer at Newark since 2001.

Newark was the first expansion brewery A-B built, back in 1951. Why build more breweries instead of expanding the home brewery in St. Louis? "We want our beer to be fresh when it gets to the consumer," Mennen said. "Where did it make sense to brew beer close to our consumers so we could get it to them that fresh? New York City is right across the river, and there's a lot of beer drinkers in the area."

Funny thing is, back in 1951, glass-lined tanks were state of the art, and that's what Newark has. Wondering where you've heard that phrase before? How about the back of a Rolling Rock bottle? When A-B bought the Rolling Rock brand from InBev in 2006, Newark was the natural choice to make the beer because of that, and it's the only place A-B makes it.

"Rolling Rock is a unique beer and flavor," Mennen said. "We had to learn a lot about the beer. We worked with their brewers, brought in their ingredients, and looked to match that flavor exactly. We brewed several trials, tested them, reviewed them, and we don't think you can tell the difference. We're very proud of the project, and proud of brewing Rolling Rock."

Rolling Rock goes nationwide, but when Bud or Bud Light rolls out of the brewery, it may be going to New York, Delaware, Pennsylvania, Rhode Island, or Connecticut. Newark is near rail lines, major highways, and the Port of Elizabeth, so this location supplies a number of domestic and international military posts as well.

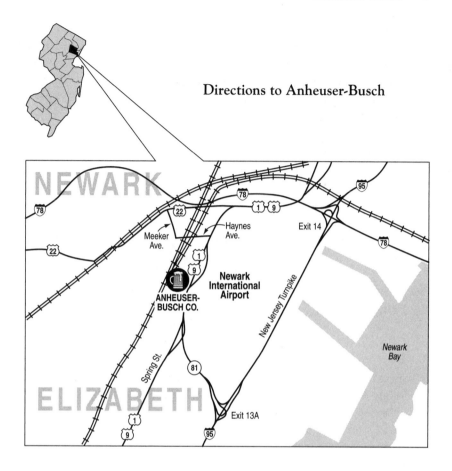

Directions to Anheuser-Busch

Of course, it also supplies New Jersey; it's a local beer, supplying local payroll. I was at the Warrenside Tavern, out in Bloomsbury, New Jersey, when I saw a Budweiser coaster in the shape of the state. The text on the coaster noted that Budweiser has been brewed fresh in New Jersey since 1951.

If you're in a bar in New Jersey and order up a Bud, is it going to be superfresh? "The average age is somewhere in the 35-day range," Mennen said. "That's why we have the 'Born-On' dating. We want people to know how fresh their beer is. Look for that. That 110-day range is key."

That's why this brewery is here—to make sure New Jersey's beer is fresh. It's the little things like that, the attention to detail in everything from brewing to marketing to shelf supply, that has put A-B on top of the U.S. market.

Opened: 1951.

Owners: Anheuser-Busch Companies, Incorporated, August A. Busch IV, president.

Brewer: Scott Mennen, senior resident brewmaster.

System: Three 630-barrel kettles and two 1,100-barrel kettles in two separate brewhouses; kettles were fabricated to an A-B–specified design. Approximately 7.5 million barrels annual capacity.

Production: 7.5 million barrels in 2006.

Tours: Not available. Tours are available at other Anheuser-Busch breweries in St. Louis, Missouri; Fairfield, California; Fort Collins, Colorado; Jacksonville, Florida; and Merrimack, New Hampshire.

Area attractions: The major attractions here are *Liberty State Park* (www.libertystatepark.com) and the *Circle Line* ferries (866-782-8834, www.statueoflibertyferry.com) to *Ellis Island* (201-435-9499, www.ellisisland.com) and *Statue of Liberty* (www.nps.gov/stli). We'll assume you know about Ellis Island's fantastic computerized assistance in tracing your immigrant family roots, the great museum in the base of the Statue of Liberty, and the incredible views of New York Harbor from the Lady's feet. Liberty State Park is about open space and the *Liberty Science Center* (201-200-1000, www.lsc.org), a great science museum with a huge IMAX theater. You might also want to venture into Newark for some great eats in the *Ironbound District,* southeast of Newark Penn Station. This neighborhood hustles and bustles during the day and eats well at night in a huge variety of Latin restaurants: Brazilian, Portuguese, Spanish, Ecuadoran, as well as Italian. Check out the Ironbound website (www.go ironbound.com) for dining and shopping suggestions. One other place to check out is *Calandra's* bakery (204 First Avenue, 973-484-5598), where you can get fresh donuts, cannoli, and delicious, crusty bread; I buy Calandra's bread down here outside of Philly, and it's a family favorite.

Other area beer sites: The *Barrow Street Bar and Grill* (292 Barrow Street, Jersey City, 201-946-1411) is a nice corner bar, tucked away on a relatively quiet residential street in Jersey City. It may seem like just another place, but there are some surprises, like the house-made soups and sauces, the hardwood and quarry tile floors, free Wi-Fi, and occasional live music. It has a small beer selection, but more than the usual majors. Take some time, people-watch through the big wraparound windows, and try the classic thin-crust pizza. *Helmer's Café* (1036 Washington Street, Hoboken, 201-963-3333) has come back after a nasty fire, and Hoboken seemed pretty happy about it when I stopped in at this marvelous little gem of a German restaurant and bar; half the people at the bar were talking about how nice the place looked after the renovations. Well and good, but how's the beer? Excellent, I'm happy to say, with some uncommon German taps (Ettaler Kloster Dunkel and Reissdorf were on that day), some good crafts, and a surprising pair of Belgians. The selection of spirits, and their preparation in cocktails, matched that level, and the food was *ausgezeichnet* (superb). A wonderfully civilized oasis, found on a busy, cosmopolitan street, that is reason enough on its own to visit Hoboken.

Beer Traveling

First things first: "Beer traveling" is not about driving drunk from brewpub to brewpub. Beer outings are similar to the wine trips celebrated in glossy travel and food magazines; they're pleasant combinations of carefree travel and the semimystical enjoyment of a potion in its birthplace. To be sure, the vineyards of France may be more hypnotically beautiful than the close-set streets of the Oranges, but you can't get Taylor Ham in the Rhône Valley, either. Life's a series of trade-offs.

Beer traveling is sometimes the only way to taste limited-release brews or brewpub beers. Beer is usually fresher at bars and distributors near the source. And the beer you'll get at the brewery itself is sublimely fresh, beer like you'll never have it anywhere else—the supreme quaff. You'll also get a chance to see the brewing operations and maybe talk to the brewer.

One of the things a beer enthusiast has to deal with is the perception that beer drinkers are second-class citizens compared with wine and single-malt scotch connoisseurs. Announcing plans for a vacation in the Napa Valley or a couple of weeks on Scotland's Whisky Trail might arouse envious glances. A vacation built around brewery tours, on the other hand, might generate only mild confusion or pity. Microbreweries sell T-shirts and baseball caps, and beer geeks wear them. I've never seen a Beringer "Wine Rules!" T-shirt or a Chandon gimme cap. Beer-related souvenirs are plastic "beverage wrenches" and decorated pint glasses. Wine paraphernalia tends to be of a higher order: corkscrews, foil cutters, tasting glasses.

How do you as a beer enthusiast deal with this problem of perception? Simple: Revel in it. The first time Lew's family went on a long camping trip with an experienced camper friend, they were concerned about wearing wrinkled clothes and sneakers all the time. The guide had one reply to all the worries: "Hey! You're campers! Enjoy it!" It worked for them, it will work for you: "Hey! I'm traveling to breweries!" How bad can that be?

When you're planning a beer outing, you need to think about your approach. If you want to visit just one brewery, you can settle in at a nearby hotel. Get your walking shoes ready, and you're set to work your way through the offerings. But this is New Jersey, the land of the driver, where almost everything is a few miles of often complicated routes apart. If you plan to visit several breweries or bars in different towns, it is essential that you travel with a nondrinking driver.

You should know that the beer at brewpubs and microbreweries is sometimes stronger than mainstream beer. Often brewers will tell you the alcohol content of their beers. Pay attention to it. Keep in mind that most mainstream beers are between 4.5 and 5 percent ABV, and judge your limits accordingly. Of course, you might want to do your figuring before you start sampling.

About that sampling: You'll want to stay as clear-headed as possible, both during the day so you can enjoy the beer and the morning after so you can enjoy life. The best thing to do is drink water. Every pro we know swears by it. If you drink a pint of water for every 2 pints of beer you drink (1 to 1 is even better), you'll enjoy the beer more during the day. Drinking that much water slows down your beer consumption, which is a good thing. Drinking that much water also helps keep away the *katzenjammers*, as the Germans call the evil spirits that cause hangovers. Just remember that if you do, you'll probably also want to follow the sage advice apocryphally attributed to President Ulysses S. Grant: "Never pass up an opportunity to urinate." There is, however, no substitute for the simple strategy of drinking moderate amounts of beer in the first place.

Beer traveling is about enjoying beer and discovering the places where it is at its best. You could make a simple whirlwind tour of breweries, but we suggest you do other things too; that's why we've included them. We've always enjoyed trips to breweries more when we mixed in other attractions. Beer is only part of life, after all.

Megalopolis

The city of New York has cast its long shadow over the neighboring region since colonial times. The megalopolis stretches from Western Connecticut to North Central New Jersey.

At one time, New York City was the place to live, but as vacant real estate began to disappear, options for residing in the city became not only scarcer, but also more expensive. Many of those who worked or did business in the city no longer wanted to reside on a busy street that stayed awake all night. Those with families wanted to buy their own homes and have some space to raise their kids. Suburbia became the destination for those who could afford it.

Even as the boroughs and outlying areas swelled with those looking for places to live, the logical move was across the Hudson River into New Jersey. Large commuter developments began to crop up all over the northern section of the state. Many of the cities of the North already had their own set of problems coping with the growing immigrant populations and could not handle a major influx of New Yorkers. As people realized they could get more bang for their buck across the river, a greater exodus of the upper middle class found its way to "suburban" New York. The sprawl began to spread farther and farther into the rural and shore areas. Today anywhere within a one- to two-hour commute is considered reasonable.

This move did not go unnoticed by the industrial community. Businesses realized that the prospects for getting the best of both worlds—owning sufficient property to build a large enough facility while still having easy access to both metropolitan New York and Philadelphia—would allow their enterprises to grow. This brought even more commerce to the areas near to the city. Places like Edison, Jersey City, and Hoboken grew with the expansion.

With the growth of the industrial complexes came the workforces that were needed to fuel them. Cities once again experienced an influx of people who wanted to live near their jobs. Some of the smaller towns not already bedroom communities for New York City and Newark were not quite prepared for this revolutionary growth and were presented with a myriad of problems in providing services. Housing projects sprang up and ethnic ghettos took root in many of the cities. Governments coped with these situations and learned some hard lessons while they did.

But with the movement came local commerce. Businessmen opened ethnic stores, and neighborhood taverns became meeting places just like in the "Old Country." Industries of all kinds evolved to handle the cultural needs of the cross-river immigrants. Food suppliers produced or imported the ethnic ingredients demanded by their residents, breweries were built to supply the locals, and the neighborhoods began to become little cities of their own.

A few questions remained. Now that all these industries had settled in the Garden State, and its largest market was New York, how did one get from here to there efficiently? This has been a problem since the founding of the colonies. No matter how many roads, bridges, or tunnels are built, there never seem to be enough to handle the crush of daily traffic. The Garden State Parkway was built to connect both ends of the state in the east and the New Jersey Turnpike to connect the southern United States with the Northeast as I-95. The planners of these roads back in the 1950s could not foresee the amount of traffic these roads would have to contend with today. Traveling on the Garden State Parkway from South to North Jersey really illustrates the differences between the two regions. After traversing the Pine Barrens in the south, the industrial feel of the north prevails. Upon crossing the Raritan Bridges, traffic swells considerably and the exits come fast and furious, with cities whose names have become synonymous with their exit number. Even so, the megalopolis rules: All roads here at one point or another will take you to New York.

The still large number of commuters entering and exiting the metropolis daily taxes all these systems that were built so many years ago. Our love of the automobile has clogged our highways and byways for decades and is especially poignant in a city like New York, where traffic is ubiquitous and parking is nigh to impossible to find or exorbitantly expensive. Many ride the trains and buses that cross the Hudson, and they too are sometimes overwhelmed by the sea of commuters. The railroad infrastructure was built many decades ago, with few to no major upgrades in all that time.

New York City may have been the catalyst that helped fuel this unprecedented growth in North Jersey, but the maintenance of this expansion has been kept alive by the communities themselves. Cities need to keep their economies growing and their tax base viable. They're always looking to attract new industry into their jurisdiction to feed the ever-expanding budgets. These businesses draw from the highly skilled workforce available here, which lessens the drain on already meager unemployment resources. At the same time, they find New Jersey to be a great place to grow their enterprise. Everybody wins.

This industrialized section of the Garden State surely does not live up to the state's nickname. Between the factories, office buildings, and overcrowded cities, it has more concrete, steel, and asphalt than grass or forests. The picture everyone has of northern New Jersey is one of a large Superfund site exploited by the petrochemical companies.

This is not an accurate representation of the region. True, a multitude of refineries and chemical plants still operate in the area, but governmental oversight has improved things tremendously. The relocation of these complexes would be prohibitively expensive, so here they remain until technology advances enough to make them obsolete. The economy of the region depends on these industries for existence, and any major changes would spell doom for an entire community.

We sometimes forget that while this region is the hub of industry, it is also the center of art, culture, and sports for the state. The bridges and tunnels let not only people cross, but also their diverse customs and ethnic talents. Museums, cultural centers, art galleries, restaurants, and stores all permeate these urban areas. The New Jersey Center for the Performing Arts in Holmdel has a long list of events of all kinds— music, dance, theater. Even several New York City teams play on the Jersey side of the Hudson at the Meadowlands.

There are still oases not far from the industrial complexes. To the west in the Skylands region of the state, it's a different world indeed, but commuters continue to make the long journey into the Big Apple every day. Real estate prices soar, and with them the tax rate; those who spent their lives in these communities can no longer afford to live there. The shadow grows longer . . .

But do not despair—there is good beer to be found here. And in this aspect, the industrial north has it all over the arid south. Ever since colonial times, this region has been the center for beer production. Newark has been home to more than its share of major breweries and is still the residence of Anheuser-Busch, the largest brewery in the state. With all its history, the north has really picked up on the craft beer revolution. Good beer bars, brewpubs, and some great breweries keep the tradition flowing this side of the river. So pick your exit, get off the Parkway or Turnpike, and have a beer at a local tappie. No need to let the shadow give you tunnel vision.

Climax Brewing

112 Valley Road, Roselle Park, NJ 07204
908-620-9585
www.climaxbrewing.com, climaxbrew@aol.com

Certainly the most colorful character on the New Jersey brewing scene today is Dave Hoffmann of Climax Brewing Company in Roselle Park. Dave has an opinion on everything, particularly beer and brewing in New Jersey, and speaks his mind when asked or taken to the brink. He has been accused of having a sharp wit, which has not always made him popular with those on the opposite side of the question.

But he's not being mean-spirited, just spirited. "I try to keep quiet, but sometimes they take me too far," explained Dave. "Everybody has an opinion, but maybe I tend to be more vocal sometimes. Don't get me started on the New Jersey alcohol bureaucracy."

His outspoken demeanor is only surpassed by his assurance that his beer is the best to be found anywhere. Lack of confidence is not a problem with Dave—and with good reason. He started out as an owner of a homebrew shop, The Brewmeister, in Cranford and worked as a brewing consultant for Gold Coast Brewing Company. His father, Kurt, owned a tool-and-die shop and had some unused space in the rear of it. Dave suggested they install a brewery there. He had a custom brewing system constructed and opened his brewery with nothing more than a dream and the support of his father. Thus began the microbrewery revolution in the Garden State.

This dream has grown into a successful business with limited statewide distribution—self-distribution, I might add. Dave is his own best salesman; who could extol his beer's virtues better than he? "Nobody knows more about my products

Beers brewed: Year-round: IPA, Extra Special Bitter Ale, Nut Brown Ale, Cream Ale. Seasonals and occasionals: Helles, Doppel Bock, Wheat Ale, Barleywine.

than I do," proclaimed Dave. "Besides, I'm already on the payroll."

He maintains two brands under the Climax banner: Climax and Hoffmann. The Climax brands are ales and the Hoffmann brands are lagers. Easy, right?

On the recently produced DVD, *American Beer,* Dave explains his lifetime connection with beer. Kurt, you see, is from Germany and raised his son on *guten Bier.* "Dad always had good German beers around the house, so I was weaned on the likes of Dinkelacker, Monchshof, and DAB. I never liked the American light lagers, so I decided to learn to homebrew so I could keep myself and my father supplied with good beers. Most people would brew one or two beers a month, but I would do three or four in a day, so I always had a lot of beer on tap at my house. I love beer!"

Strangely enough, with all the background in traditional German beers, the first brews out of the kettle were classic English styles: ESB, Porter, IPA, and Nut Brown Ale. These have remained his flagship products for the past eleven years. Most of his seasonals and specialties, however, are of German extraction. For the brewery's tenth anniversary, Dave brewed his first barleywine. As he's an aficionado of session beers, this was a bit out of the ordinary for him. I was present when he gave a sample to Michael Jackson for his opinion. The Beerhunter gave his seal of approval, as did I. A definite success, and now a beer Dave will make for every anniversary. He also presented me with a bottle to squirrel away for a snowy day . . . still waiting for that blizzard!

One of the most unusual aspects of this brewery is that they bottle in half-gallon growler jugs. Besides Dave's kegged offerings, this is the only way you can purchase his products. "We didn't want to have to purchase a very expensive bottling system," he said, "so we built a six-head counterpressure growler filler to do the job. It performs as efficiently as anything we could have purchased."

At six growlers every forty-five seconds, it's not state of the art, but then again, they're not bottling several hundred thousand of them either. Besides, Dave and Kurt get to drink the overflow, and by the time they're done, they're riding a pretty good buzz and the day has just sailed by.

Using a half-gallon bottle presents its own set of obstacles. One is the need for larger labels to identify the product and satisfy the government requirements. Longtime friend and fellow beer lover Gregg Hinlicky does all the logo and label work for Climax. (Gregg also did the wall murals at both locations of Basil T's.)

The Pick: Not an easy choice, but the final call is the ESB, a delicious all-day drinker with beautiful malt character. Hoist that half-gallon high!

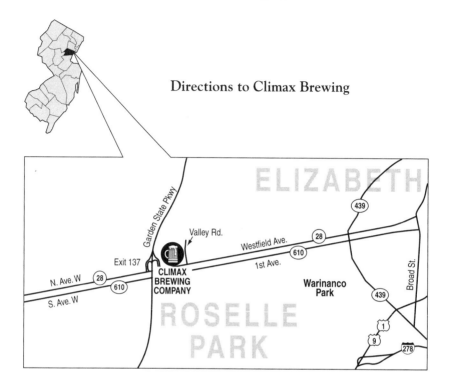

Directions to Climax Brewing

Another problem is that retailers don't like to stock that large a container; it takes up too much shelf space. Dave has a few questions for those retailers who won't: "I don't understand. You sell all those %&*#! Belgian beers in weird-size bottles; what's the problem with an American beer in a weird-size bottle? I don't have that weird mystique? I don't make sour, awful-tasting beer, or what? Besides, my half-gallon of beer costs less than $10, certainly a lot less than those imports!"

How can one argue with such logic? The product is of the highest quality, made with the best ingredients you can buy, and being sold for a reasonable price. What difference would a little space make?

Twelve years in business is a testament to his attention to quality. So many breweries have come and gone in a lot less time, something that will continue to transpire as long as there are people not committing themselves to excellence of product.

Ready to make the trek to Roselle Park? Call first to be sure someone is there. Dave and Kurt spend time on the road delivering, and several days a week, Dave is minding the kettles at Basil T's Toms River.

Finding the brewery is a whole other story. From the front, it looks like an abandoned building; you need to go to the rear for all the action. A couple days a week, Dave and Kurt can be found brewing, bottling, sanitizing tanks, or cleaning. If you're lucky, Dave might have something in the tank and will give you a taste. Of course, it will only be a small taste, as New Jersey law precludes his pouring anything but. "I can't even *sell* my beer out of the brewery without another license, and I'd have to collect the tax on it too!"

Well, if you've never had a Climax (whew . . .), look for those growlers at your local retailer. If you can't find them, ask for them. It'll be the best $10 you ever spent!

Opened: June 1994.
Owners: Kurt and Dave Hoffmann.
Brewer: Dave Hoffmann.
System: 15-barrel Pub System, 4,000-barrel annual capacity.
Production: Approximately 1,000 barrels in 2006.
Tours: By appointment only.
Take-out beer: Not available.
Special considerations: Kids welcome. Handicapped-accessible.
Parking: Lot on property.
Lodging in the area: Kenilworth Inn, 60 South 31st Street, Kenilworth, 908-241-4100; Homewood Suites, 2 Jackson Drive, Cranford, 908-709-1980; Clarktowne Inn, 70 Central Avenue, Clark, 732-381-6076.
Area attractions: *Galloping Hill Golf Course,* 21 North 31st Street, Kenilworth, 908-686-1556; *Oak Ridge Country Golf Course,* 136 Oak Ridge Road, Clark, 732-574-0139. See the listings for Anheuser-Busch also.
Other area beer sites: If you're looking for Dave's beers on tap, go to *Antone's Tap* (112 South Avenue East, Cranford, 908-276-3414), just a hop, skip, and a jump away from the brewery. It is a rustic neighborhood bar in downtown Cranford, with wood-paneled walls and trophy fish protruding from them. It's a great place to get together with friends and enjoy a good meal and beer. The menu is surprisingly sophisticated for a small establishment. Not a very large space, so you can't help but get to know the guy sitting next to you at the bar. Oh, and they also have thirty taps full of good craft beer; Climax Brewing usually occupies three or four of them. Dave also makes their house beer. Just down the street is a branch of *The Office* (3 South Avenue, West, Cranford, 908-272-3888). Some of you may know that I've got a rant about chain restaurants at my website (www.lewbryson.com), and that I think they're a sign of the Apocalypse. Well, if the Apocalypse has gotta come, I can

think of much worse signs for it than The Office. This chain of beer bars is spreading through central and northern Jersey. They have a good tap selection, although they could do a lot better on local crafts. Each place also has a deep bottle list, and—a very good sign—there are no typos and only one or two errors. The menu is a step above the usual, too, and the atmosphere did not have the cookie-cutter, get 'em in and get 'em out vibe that makes me feel so less than welcome at so many places. If The Office is what it takes to bring better beer variety to New Jersey, I'll swallow my chain anger . . . and another well-kept pint, please. Let's be honest: **Jake and Jocco's Riverside Inn** (56 North Avenue, Cranford, 908-276-9783) isn't much to look at, inside or out, the beer's only a notch above average, and the parking's a pain (do *not* park in the lot right beside it!). The locals don't call it "the Dive" for nothing (actually, that's what they called the place that was in the building before, and the name stuck). But the place has an authenticity to it, a character, that's real New Jersey: a comfortable, contradictory mixture of used, ageless cynicism with the pure open friendliness of a puppy. That, and the burgers are truly good. Try these for take-home: **Shop-Rite Liquors** (333 South Avenue, East, Westfield, 908-232-8700) and **Roselle Park Liquors** (Chestnut Street, Roselle Park, 908-245-2333).

Cricket Hill Brewing Company

24 Kulick Road, Fairfield, NJ 07004
973-276-9415
www.CricketHillBrewery.com

Cricket Hill? Bugs and beer . . . what could possibly be the connection there? Chirp for a beer? Founder, owner, and brewer Rick Reed revealed the idea behind the name: "If you're a bloke who wants to have a pint of beer and sit with the larrikins, you have to sit on the cricket hill." Don't ask me, I just wrote what he said. He further explained that one of the largest per capita beer consumers in the world is the country from "down under," and that they play cricket possibly for days on end. I gather that the "cricket hill" must be a place to sit and observe the proceedings of the game while enjoying a couple of cold ones with the boys. Where a guy from Pittsburgh came up with such an Aussie witticism, I can't tell you, but he has certainly come up with a good beer philosophy and a great lineup of brews.

Rick figured that beer drinkers were getting bored with the usual offerings from the Bud-Miller-Coors camp and were looking for an alternative that wasn't too strong or hoppy but wasn't too light either, so he thought he'd pursue the Step 1 philosophy: "Because New Jersey is behind the bell curve, Cricket Hill products are the first step above the industrial lagers and can make for an easy transition from them to more flavorful choices," he explained. "A 300 percent growth rate in the last few years certainly vindicates my belief in that idea."

I couldn't agree more. There's a lot to be said for that sector of the market. A plethora of beers on the shelves miss that target demographic. Rick uses his advertising to make the fact known that he's seeking these folks as customers. What with all the over-the-top and esoteric beers flooding the market, beer consumers who seek to find a crossover beer are left scratching their heads while wandering down row upon row of domestic and import beers at their local stores. No wonder many just give up and stick with "Old Faithful." At least they know what to expect.

But that is not to say that Cricket Hill wants to leave the beer geeks out of the loop. "I don't believe that everyone wants to drink a super-lupulin-infused or 15 percent ABV beer all the time," Rick said. "I try to fill the bill when a session beer is called for . . . sitting around with friends watching the game or after mowing the lawn, for example."

Resting on his laurels is not Rick's style either, and the company has instituted some changes that will expand their lineup of bottled and draft beers. Colonel Blides Bitter was once a draft-only offering, but it will now be bottled as a flagship beer all year round. A new summer seasonal called Jersey Summer, a Belgian-style breakfast ale, also will be joining the ranks. It's a wonderfully spicy and fruity brew, with hints of banana, cloves, and bubble gum usually found in the Belgian wits and

Beers brewed: Year-round: East Coast Lager, American Ale, Hopnotic IPA, Colonel Blide's Bitter. Seasonals: Fall Festival Ale, Paymasters Porter, Jersey Summer Breakfast Ale, My Oh Mybock.

The Pick: Colonel Blide's Bitter. Call me predictable, but I'm just a sucker for a good session beer, and I was happy to hear that Rick had decided to take Colonel Blide's year-round recently. I remember my first sip: clean, firmly malty while still lightly drinkable, and a great finish that releases your mouth only on the promise that you'll have another sip. Sah! Colonel Blide reporting for duty, sah!

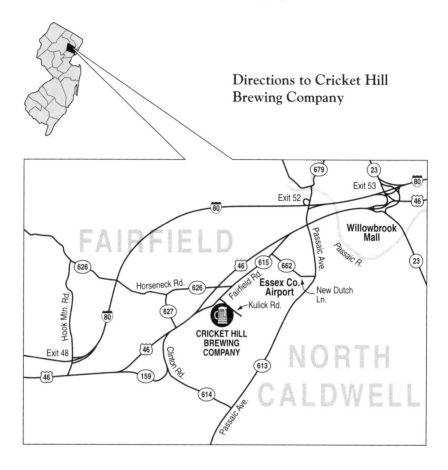

Directions to Cricket Hill
Brewing Company

German weissbiers, but this offering is made without the wheat. The yeast imparts the beer with that flavor profile and would confound the most trained palate.

Cricket Hill holds open houses on a regular basis, allowing fans and new recruits to come into the brewery and enjoy several samples of their products. This is one way to acquaint people with your beers and let the crew that brews them introduce themselves to the public. Giving your beer a face has been a tried-and-true marketing method, in hopes that people will remember you when they're in the store looking over the wide selection of beers available. Visitors always enjoy a tour of the brewery, and it's a good method for recruiting volunteers to help out. Running a small brewery can be labor-intensive, and free (or at least cheap) labor can really help the bottom line.

Another one of Rick's programs has his beer in several local ballparks. East Coast Lager is a big hit with the baseball crowd and sells a good bit of beer at the stadiums. "I'm hoping that the growth in this market will continue to expand and we'll be available in more stadiums throughout the state," he said. "Baseball and local beer has a long history behind it, not only in New Jersey, but nationwide. I think it's a great matchup. We try to participate in all the events held at the parks to keep us visible."

Tucked away in an industrial park in Fairfield, the brewery has a good bit of space for expansion as the business grows. Being in the industrial hub of North Jersey, the location is very important. Easily accessible to I-80, I-280, the New Jersey Turnpike, and Garden State Parkway, the brewery can move its products almost anywhere in the Northeast Corridor. For now, Rick is looking at bolstering his image throughout New Jersey, but I'm sure he also has expansion into other states on his mind if the markets open up.

Watch for more good things to come from this small brewery. Rick and his staff are adamant about growing this business, and they are winning over new palates every day with their well-made and tasty products. See if you can woo some of your BMC (that's "Bud, Miller, and Coors") drinking friends over to the realm of better beer with the Step 1 philosophy from Cricket Hill.

Opened: December 2000.
Owner: Rick Reed.
Brewer: David Manka.
System: 15-barrel Criveller system, 3,500 barrels annual capacity.
Production: 1,000 barrels in 2006.
Tours: Fridays, 5 P.M. to 7 P.M.
Take-out beer: Two six-packs per person per visit, state maximum.
Special considerations: Kids welcome. Handicapped-accessible.
Parking: On-site lot.
Lodging in the area: Holiday Inn Select, 111 West Main Street, Clinton, 908-735-5111; Riverside Victorian B&B, 66 Leigh Street, Clinton, 908-238-0400; Hampton Inn, 118 U.S. Highway 46, Fairfield, 973-575-5777.
Area attractions: Nearby Clinton was a mill town, back in the day, and the **Red Mill Museum Village** (56 Main Street, 908-735-4101, www.theredmill.org) has a beautifully restored example by the waterfall in Clinton, along with a limestone quarry, schoolhouse, and log cabin. You'll find exhibits of tools, demonstrations, and encampments by reenactors from the Civil, Revolutionary, and French and Indian Wars. On the other side of the waterfall is the

Hunterdon Museum of Art (7 Lower Center Street, 908-735-8415, www.hunterdonartmuseum.org), also in an 1800s mill building. The collection is centered on prints and also has paintings, sculpture, and photographs.

Other area beer sites: Good call, Rick Reed. Cricket Hill's owner suggested the *Cloverleaf Tavern* (395 Bloomfield Avenue, Caldwell, 973-226-9812), and he was dead on the money. The Cloverleaf is very friendly and definitely hip to the whole beer variety idea, with sixteen taps that include New Jersey beers and some crafts beyond the "usual suspects," plus a bottle selection that dropped my jaw. Don't miss the beer garden out back in warm weather, either.

Egan and Sons

118 Walnut Street, Montclair, NJ 07042
973-744-1413
www.eganandsons.com

"What about Egan and Sons?"

"Everybody I'm talking to says it's not a brewpub. They're not brewing anymore."

"I called. They said they are. I'm going to have to go check."

The two of us put in a lot of Turnpike and Parkway miles to write this book, and we did it gladly. But we're always looking to save a trip by checking status before we go. Egan and Sons was a tough call; reliable people were saying they weren't "actually" brewing, while the bartender we called at the place said yes, they were. I couldn't get Chris Egan on the phone; he was always away.

Considering their brewing system didn't make things any easier. They have a Breworx system, which is kind of halfway between a full-fledged brewery and the weird little "pour in this and just add hot water and yeast" systems that were out there in odd corners (almost all shut down now). Breworx is a set of fermenters and serving tanks and a system to send the establishments wort, the

Beers brewed: Chris has options on thirty-two different Breworx beers, and they all rotate through. There's usually some kind of lager on, a couple ales, and something a bit different. Dark beers come in the wintertime, lighter beers in the summer. "I'd like to do a ginger beer," says Chris. "They're great with food."

prefermentation liquid that just needs fermentation and a bit of aging to become beer.

I only knew of one other wort brewery, C'est What? in Toronto, but their beer's pretty damned good. Other beer geeks, however, could have a different opinion, as in "That's not brewing!" that could color their reports.

So I hopped in the car and drove to Montclair: simple, direct. Egan's is a great-looking place on a nice street, and the inside is splendid, with a long bilevel marble bar with a footrail (I love bars with footrails) and big frosted cobra taps. There's a deep spirits selection with an exceptional collection of Irish whiskey, a fair variety of wines, and a decent number of commercial beer taps and a choice of bottles my notes say was "definitely worthy." In fact, if this were just a bar, I'd recommend it and probably stick it in the book somewhere.

But it's not, because there were four taps of house beer: Lager, Oktoberfest, Red Ale, and Oddfellow Ale were on at the time. I asked for a sample and I got one: free. "Tell me which one you want after you tried them," the bartender said. Wow, okay. I settled on the Oddfellow, got my big dimple mug of it, and took a deep sip. Quite a bit better than I'd been led to believe, downright good beer and no struggle to finish.

But before I did, I saw a medium-height fellow with broad shoulders and curly gray hair walk up to the bar and get something from the bartender, who called him Chris. I asked him if he was Chris Egan, and sure enough, he was. I explained why I was there, and within two minutes we were in the snug, where I was taking rapid notes—and continuing to sip Oddfellow—as Chris explained what was going on.

You might expect anyone who'd put in something like a Breworx system to be new to craft brewing and not really hip to the whole beer thing. Dead wrong. Chris worked at Commonwealth Brewing in Boston, back in the day. Commonwealth sat right beside Boston Garden, and it was a real gold standard place, real ale all the time, open square fermenters, English ales at English temperatures and English carbonation levels, the customers' preference be damned. I remember thinking I'd died and gone to heaven the first time I visited.

That's not how Chris remembered it. "Sure, the owner did everything right," he said in his lilting brogue—Egan's a Dubliner. "But the amount of investment and space it took up, and the inability to really blow out more if one got popular . . . it just didn't make sense, and that's not what the crowd wanted when the Garden left out."

The Pick: I only got to try five beers, but of those, the Oktoberfest and Oddfellow Ale stuck out. The fest was very clean, sharp enough to cut you, with a crisp maltiness and surprising hop-catch to it, maybe a bit out of style, but good. The Oddfellow was more classic English ale, mellow and a bit fruity.

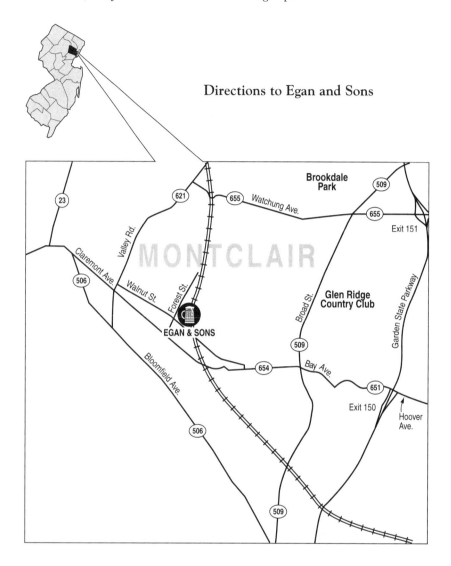

Directions to Egan and Sons

Egan didn't want that kind of problem or investment, but he still liked the idea of fresh beer. Breworx seemed perfect. "We're not looking to be pretentious," he said. "We leave our beer snobbery at the door. If they want our beer, that's great. But without that big brewery, we can afford to sell other beers. So if they just want to watch the game with a freezing cold draft light beer, we've got that too.

"The beer market's soft, but we're holding our own," he told me, with some satisfaction. "If we can provide consistency with freshness, and we can turn on a dime when we want something different, we've got it."

Egan ought to know what he's doing. He's been working in pubs since he was sixteen, in France and Switzerland, and wound up owning four pubs in Dublin. "I still have two," he said, which explained why he was always away when I tried to call. One of the pubs, the Bruxelles, is portrayed in a small sculpture on the backbar.

He's a hustler, a mover and doer. He was hanging new speakers that day. "The customers can see I've got my soul in the place," he said.

That's the key to success for Egan—that connection of innkeeper and inn that a chain place can't touch. "The future is in independents," he said. "When we want to change our menu, we do it. If we get a deal on fresh fish, it's on the menu tonight; I don't have expensive preset menus I have to ask permission to change. We listen, and we take suggestions."

He can't seem to stay in one place. As of this writing, a seafood restaurant is being built next door and upstairs, more dining space for Egan and Sons being added out back. Egan's acting as his own general contractor.

I thanked him, we shook hands, and Chris Egan was off again, hustling to get a few more things done before he changed into his sport coat and started working the front of the house. His soul's in his place.

Is it "really" a brewpub? Egan's brewer, Todd Miller, takes wort that is not beer and makes it beer on-premises. It's simplified, it's practically brew-by-numbers, but Egan's is making beer. That's good enough for me, and that's why you're reading this. Now go have a beer!

Opened: April 2005.

Owner: Chris Egan.

Brewer: Todd Miller.

System: Breworx fermentation-only system with two 100-gallon vessels; projected annual capacity of 355 barrels.

Production: Approximately 150 barrels in 2006.

Brewpub hours: Monday through Saturday, 3:30 P.M. to 1 A.M.; Sunday, 3:30 P.M. to midnight.

Tours: None offered.

Take-out beer: Half-gallon growlers.

Food: The menu shows an Irish accent, but like Ireland itself these days, it's gone uptown with it: cider-glazed salmon, "fiery" rubbed pork chops, and for fans of the BBC's "Father Ted," Craggy Island Pie, with fresh cod and mussels in a fish velouté . . . you never got this down at the pub. If you want pub grub, you can get that too, and it's delicious.

Extras: St. Patrick's Day is an extravaganza, as you might expect. Try to get the snug when you go: a special table in a small half room across from the bar in the back of the main area. The standard arrangement of sportscasting TVs hangs over the bar.

Special considerations: Kids welcome. Handicapped-accessible. Vegetarian meals available.

Parking: Free lot in the back, a wonder in Montclair.

Lodging in the area: Georgian Inn, 37 North Mountain Avenue, Montclair, 973-746-7156; Residence Inn, 107 Prospect Avenue, West Orange, 973-669-4700.

Area attractions: The **Montclair Art Museum** (3 South Mountain Avenue, 973-746-5555, www.montclairartmuseum.org) has a strong collection from the Hudson River School, a personal favorite. They also have a cool museum store.

Other area beer sites: Egan and Sons just happens to be centrally located to some of the best bars in New Jersey, at least in our experience. If you were just dropped without warning into **Tierney's Tavern** (138 Valley Road, Montclair, 973-744-9785), you might think you were up in the Skylands instead of intensely suburban Montclair. Tierney's is endearingly rough-hewn and worn, with an old wooden floor and a big racetrack bar under an old plaster ceiling with exposed beams: solid in its bones and looking almost European in its comfortable age. The beer selection is small but wisely chosen, with a welcome Cricket Hill tap, and the place is usually busy with friendly, talkative regulars. Easily one of my favorite bar visits in three months of research; I'll see you there sometime soon. There's another branch of **The Office** here too (619 Bloomfield Avenue, Montclair, 201-783-2929). I actually set up my laptop and phone and PDA at a corner table and used this as *my* office one cold afternoon when I had to do some phone interviews while I was making bar visits. Thanks to the Montclair staff for being so accommodating!

I had the best jar of Guinness I've had in months at the **Franklin Steak House** (522 Franklin Avenue, Nutley, 973-667-1755)—and believe me, boyo, I drink my fair share of it. There's a wider selection of drafts than that might lead you to believe; you won't be disappointed. Best of all, it's a classy place: long granite bar, smartly dressed staff, a nice dining room, and a wide selection of spirits. The beef, as you'd expect, is great and hardly one-dimensional: I had a Bloomfield Avenue Burger for lunch, a thick and juicy patty of fresh meat piled with fried onions and sweet red peppers and a surprise topping of fresh-made potato chips. Different and delicious.

Fitzgerald's Harp 'n Bard (363 Lakeview Avenue, Clifton, 973-772-7282) caught me completely off-guard. I was expecting just another Irish "pub," Guinness and fish and chips, begorra, whoopee. Jeez, who knew: Fitzgerald's is tremendously beer-savvy, with one of the best selection of taps I saw in the state. It's kind of plain, in a classic pub way, but with a sports-bar annex next door, and discount pints all day on Wednesday and every weekday night, I can stand a little plain.

Got another one for you railroad buffs: The **Railroad Café** (170 Union Avenue, East Rutherford, 201-939-0644) is so close to the rails you can feel the rumble, and the old, honestly worn decor is all train-related. Me, I like the old-school bar with its solid step and big, beautiful backbar. The deck outside has a nice view of Manhattan. The beer's a definite step up from standard sports-bar fare, and though I've never eaten there, the smells coming from other folks' dinners sure are appetizing. Hop off the train and have a glass.

Talk "beer bar" in New Jersey and four names always come up, and have come up for years. Firewaters, in Atlantic City, the most recent addition; the Old Bay, in New Brunswick, probably more for what it used to be under the late Chris Demetri; Haledon's quirky and beer-loving The Shepherd and the Knucklehead; and **Andy's Corner Bar** (265 Queen Anne Road, Bogota, 201-342-9887). It's a tough call, but I give Andy's the nod for longevity and selection. The taps rotate constantly, and I've heard that on occasion they're pretty average, but I've always been impressed when I visit. It's not very big, and it's sure not very fancy, but the beer's well kept and served, and the folks are friendly, talkative, and interesting. This is the local bar for *Ale Street News* publisher Tony Forder, and all I can say is that he's a lucky dog. Andy's isn't really that close to Egan's, but there was no way I was going to skip it!

Gaslight Brewery and Restaurant

15 South Orange Avenue, South Orange, NJ 07079
973-762-7077
www.gaslightbrewery.com

Now what do you get when you have a mother who's worked in the restaurant business for many years and has a son who is an avid home-brewer? A family-run brewpub, of course. "We wanted to open up a restaurant. My mother, Cynthia, has been involved in restaurants for a lot of years and wanted to open one up, and I wanted to open a brewery, so we thought that a brewpub would be a good combination," explained Dan Soboti Jr., the brewer. That's how the Soboti family opened the only brewpub in Essex County. Each member of the family has an aspect of the business to attend to and pitches in where needed.

The Gaslight has that neighborhood bar feel to it. The warm wood and brick walls with lots of breweriana make for a very familiar and comfortable decor. The neon signs, sports items, and seven TVs let you know that you'll not be missing any games here. Sitting down at the bar, I noticed something different: I didn't feel wood or metal under my butt. The seats are the most comfortable I've ever sat on in a pub setting, nicely upholstered and soft to keep the bottom from tiring during those long beer sessions or overtime games.

Looking around, you spy the "wall of shame," an extensive collection hung on the wall for all to see of confiscated driver's licenses that didn't pass the reality test—a grim reminder that technology doesn't always work . . . or does it? This game of cat and mouse has taken on a whole new twist with ever more advanced technology to detect the seemingly "perfect" phonies. Gotta expect that in a college town. Seton Hall University is just a mug's throw away. Good to see the new generation is at least trying to get better beer.

It seems that brewpubs always put the brewing system in the front window like a large advertisement that real beer is produced here, but that's

Beers brewed: Year-round: Bulldog Blonde Ale, Pirate Pale Ale, Bison Brown Ale, Perfect Stout. Seasonals: 1920's Lager, Black Bear Lager, Triple 7's, Damian, Eliminator, Zum Altdorf, 3 Ring IPA, E.S.B., Hopfest, Satan Claws, Oktoberfest, Slalom Ale, Summer Solstice, Kölsch, Oatmeal Stout, Prince of Darkness, Organic Pumpkin Ale, IPA, Pinhead Pilsner, Abbey Normal.

only half the story at Gaslight. The table talkers speak volumes, telling a tale of outstanding guest taps, bottled beers, and ciders available for your enjoyment. Even if you would rather opt for something other than the house beers, the Sobotis offer the best beers you can find anywhere. On top of all that, every week something populates the hand-pump for the real ale enthusiasts. "We rotate that through our own and if I can get someone else's. It's not always easy. Several months ago, we got a cask of Stone Ruination. It was gone in less than an hour!" Now that is real (ale) love.

The Pick: I poured Gaslight's beers several years at the Garden State Craft Brewers Guild Festival, and I really enjoyed the 1920's Lager. Unlike Lew, I'm not a big lager fan, but this was quite refreshing and had a nice, balanced profile. Another great selection was the 3 Ring IPA, a homage to the Original Ballantine IPA, which was before my time—at least, my beer-drinking time. (I do remember Ballantine XXX, which my father used to let me sip.) Dan seems to have great success with these historical representations.

Upstairs is where all the special action is, with a banquet room and the U-Brew Homebrew Shop. Dan keeps a supply of homebrew paraphernalia and ingredients on hand and is always willing to give professional advice for those who are looking to brew something new and interesting.

Besides the beer dinners conducted in this private space, it's also where the local Beer Appreciation Society, The Draft Board 15, meets the second Sunday of every month. At these regular sessions, they pass around the homebrew, odd beers that members find on their quests, or just hang out and drink whatever is on tap at the brewpub. Guest speakers, recipe trading, and discussions on the latest homebrew methods and technology are regular listings on the agenda of each meeting. Several times a year, brewoffs are organized to pit the homebrewers in the group against each other. "We pick a certain style. Everybody gets the same ingredients, and then you're allowed to make it however you want. It's amazing the differences you get when you change hop additions, mashing schedules, etc.," explained the brewer. "Everyone gets to enjoy sampling them all after they're done." Every once in a while, they load up a bus and make an excursion to a variety of events, such as TAP New York at Hunter Mountain in April and Riverfront Stadium to watch the Newark Bears play. BBQ, beers, and baseball . . . the all-American outing!

The biggest event of the year is the Victorian Christmas Dinner. Here they serve up beers, wines, and sometimes meads to match up with all the special foods the chef prepares. Dan's very popular Satan Claws Barleywine is an eagerly anticipated selection at this time of year. It has received accolades from the locals and national reviewing sites.

If you can't find something on their menu, you should just stay home and fix your own. I don't think there's anything that's *not* on the list:

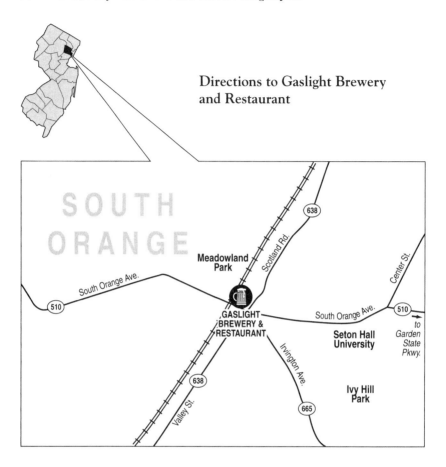

Directions to Gaslight Brewery
and Restaurant

pizza; wraps; burgers; sandwiches; Italian, Bavarian, and Creole-Cajun items. During Oktoberfest, a full German menu is offered, with all the classic selections you'd expect. But what's so special about this place? So many of the items are made on-premises. "The fresh beer goes along with the fresh food. All the food has received great reviews, because we make much of it here. We bake our own bread, make our own pickles, smoke some of the meats, make our own pastrami and corned beef, and all the desserts are prepared here. We do everything really well," boasted Dan. You don't see a lot of that these days.

So be sure to stop in at the only brewpub in Essex County and enjoy a "family" experience. Just like Mama used to make.

Opened: June 1998.
Owners: Daniel, Cynthia, Antonio, and Daniel Jr. Soboti.
Brewer: D. J. Soboti Jr.

System: 8-barrel Pub Brewing system, approximately 1,800-barrel capacity.

Production: 650 barrels in 2006.

Restaurant hours: Monday and Tuesday, 3 P.M. to midnight; Wednesday through Sunday, 11:30 A.M. to midnight. Bar is open until 2 A.M.

Tours: By appointment.

Take-out beer: Growlers and sixth-, quarter-, and half-barrel kegs.

Food: Eclectic mix of pub grub and Bavarian, Italian, and Cajun specialties. A very substantial menu including wraps, burgers, sandwiches, pizza, and pasta with lots of homemade items . . . breads, pickles, desserts, and they even smoke their own meats. Portions are large and prices reasonable.

Extras: Full bar with an exceptional wine and liquor assortment, plus ciders on tap and in the bottle and an impressive list of bottled beers and guest beers on tap. Darts and shuffleboard. NFL Ticket for Sunday games. Beer dinners several times a year.

Special considerations: Kids welcome. Vegetarian meals available. Handicapped-accessible.

Parking: Street parking and nearby garages.

Lodging in the area: Broad Street Hotel, 111 South Orange Avenue, South Orange, 973-762-2647; Turtle Brook Inn, 555 Northfield Avenue, West Orange, 973-731-5300.

Area attractions: *Seton Hall* basketball, anyone? Build a visit around a game; tickets are available at www.shupirates.com. Other campus activities, lectures, and so on, are posted at www.shu.edu. The *Turtle Back Zoo* (560 Northfield Avenue, West Orange, 973-731-7732) is in the South Mountain Reservation wildlife preserve and has a new black bear habitat, a reptile house, and a newly renovated Wolf Woods exhibit. There are 150 restaurants within 2 miles of Gaslight. The diverse demographics of the area have resulted in an eclectic array of ethnic restaurants, ranging from simple snack places to gourmet Italian, Caribbean, Japanese, Ethiopian, Chinese, German, Mexican, Indian . . . All I can say is bring your appetites. Two of the more interesting ones are *Harrar Ethiopian Café* (11 Village Plaza, South Orange, 973-761-5222) and *Café Arugula* (59 South Orange Avenue, South Orange, 973-378-9099).

Other area beer sites: Above the brewery is the U-Brew Homebrew Shop. You can find all your homebrewing needs right here while you enjoy the Soboti family's beers and food. *Cryan's Beef and Ale House* (24 1st Street, South Orange, 973-763-7114) is a solid Irish joint, with the food, the beer, and the whiskey you'd be expecting. Also see the entries for *Egan and Son's.*

Harvest Moon Brewery

392 George Street, New Brunswick, NJ 08901
732-249-6666
www.harvestmoonbrewery.com

College towns always seem to attract great places to hang out. Not only does the institution supply a built-in workforce, but when classes are in session, it provides a large customer base to boot. "Being in a college town (taking into account demographics) filled with younger crowds that live off of commercial beer, it is my job to be a transitional brewer . . . to transition the common beer drinker to the real flavor of beer, promote better beer, and respect beer of any style. Get 'em while they're young," said Matt McCord, the brewer at Harvest Moon Brewery.

New Brunswick is home to the largest campus of Rutgers University, with more than thirty-four thousand students as well as corporate giant Johnson and Johnson. The vibrant downtown area bustles with students and businesspeople going about their daily tasks. Where does one stop to partake of some good food and drink after the chores are done? Sitting right in the middle of all of this hubbub is the Harvest Moon Brewery/Café. Serving up a wide array of foods and freshly brewed beers or your favorite cocktail or wine, this venue has been satisfying the appetites and thirsts of the populace since 1996.

The shining stainless steel tanks glistening in the sunlight in the front window tell you right off that fresh beer is made here. A short saunter to the bar or a table soon proves that it is served here also. Under Matt's able direction, the brewery ferments a mind-boggling assortment of styles. There are usually eight to ten beers on tap at all times, which even makes the tasting of the sampler an event.

Here is a guy that has more energy than any two people I know, which may explain his prolificness. "I love to brew and enjoy making as many styles as I can every year," he said. "As long as the customers

Beers brewed: Year-round: British Nut Brown, Elmes Mild Manor, Full Moon Pale Ale, Hops2 Double IPA, Jimmy D's Firehouse Red Ale, Moonlight Ale, Moonshine Barleywine. Seasonals: Matt produces an impressive list of seasonals and specialties throughout the year, such as Siberian Express Imperial Stout, Oktoberfest, Spiced Winter Warmer, Harvest Hefeweizen, Lunar Eclipse Black Lager, Pumpkin Ale, Belgian Tripel, Witbier, Oatmeal Stout, Kilt Lifter Wee Heavy Scotch Ale, Roggen Lager, Mumblin' Monk Belgian Strong Ale.

keep drinking it, I'll keep brewing it. Harvest Moon has given me the opportunity to create and use my skills, use trial and error, and define and refine many styles of beer.

"When making beer, most of all, I think of drinkability," he explained. "That is why my style revolves around session beer. I know this seems against the present trend of high-powered, super-alpha beer, but I like to focus on quality and balance. And when it comes down to it, that is what I think people ultimately want. Especially in a brew-pub atmosphere, when food and good company are taken into consideration."

But does he have a philosophy on beer? "I believe that beer is the most versatile beverage known to man," he said. "I also believe there is an occasion and type of food that can be paired with any type of beer. Even if someone does not like beer, you can find one that would suit their liking in some way." Certainly many brewpub brewers have reiterated such viewpoints as the secret to success for them.

Keeping up with the seasonal eddies is another predicament of the college-town brewer. Long holiday breaks and summers bring a noticeable ebb in the flow of customers. Then when school restarts, the rush is on, and Matt is hell-bent just to keep enough beer on to cover demand. "For several months, especially in the fall, I'm working long days to keep the taps full. It's also the time of the big seasonal beers, which may have lengthy fermentation schedules," Matt said. "Oktoberfest, Pumpkin Ale, Spiced Winter Warmer, Imperial Stout . . . great winter beers, but more labor-intensive also."

Harvest Moon has an open-door policy in place: When nice weather prevails, they open the doors to the street and let the sights and sounds of downtown in. Nothing like finding a nice table by the street, contemplating a good beer, and doing "sociological research," watching the world go by on a beautiful day. Even when the weather is not so nice and your view is through the glass doors, knocking back a winter warmer while observing those battling the elements from your ringside seat is not a bad thing.

The owners and staff find that being part of the community and helping local charities is a very important part of doing business in New Brunswick. When tragedy struck the local fire department in September 2004 and Deputy Chief James D'Heron lost his life in the line of

The Pick: You must be kidding! Pick a favorite out of all these fantastic beers? Well, I guess if you really pinned me down, I'd have to say that the Elmes Mild Manor jumps out just ahead of the Hops2 Double IPA. I love my hops, but I've come to appreciate milds as a session style. The smooth, lightly roasted malt profile is not palate-searing and lends itself to a more diverse food pairing.

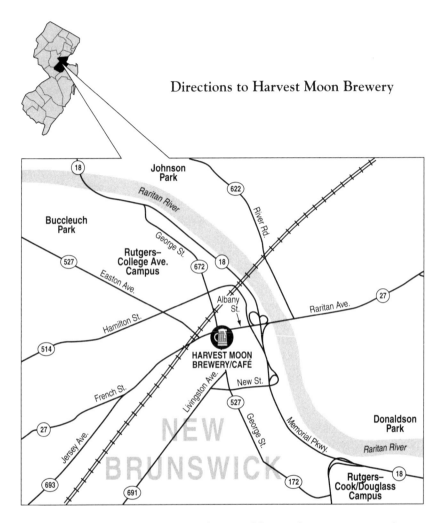

Directions to Harvest Moon Brewery

duty, Matt and the crew stepped up and brewed Jimmy D's Firehouse Red Ale. For every pint sold, Harvest Moon contributes a portion to the Children's Burn Camp of the Connecticut Burns Care Foundation. The camp helps juvenile burn victims learn to cope with their situation and enjoy themselves for a week with others in similar circumstances. The campaign has shown that you can make a difference.

Chef Michael DeAngelis is affectionately known as "Tank" to all those that know him and some that don't. Keeping both executives and college kids happy with the menu choices is not the easiest task in the world, but the kitchen seems to handle the assignment with aplomb. From the simplest of appetizers to the most elegant entrées, Tank's staff seeks to impress the customers with their culinary prowess.

The city of New Brunswick has a storied history of brewing that goes back as far as the mid-1700s. Being only 15 miles from the mouth of the Raritan River, it became the hub of commerce in the region both by boat and later by train. The beer could easily be shipped to New York City and other local ports for distribution. The last brewery to do business in New Brunswick was New Brunswick Brewing Company, which ceased operations in 1938. Harvest Moon proudly carries on this tradition.

Shine on, Harvest Moon!

Opened: 1996.

Owners: Neil Glass, Frank Kropf Jr., and Michael Elmes.

Brewer: Matt McCord.

System: 10-barrel JV Northwest system, 1,000 barrels annual capacity.

Production: 850 barrels.

Brewpub hours: Seven days a week, 11:30 A.M. to 1:30 A.M.

Tours: By appointment only.

Take-out beer: Half-gallon growlers.

Food: The owners consider the cuisine to be contemporary American gastropub style. The kitchen is headed up by Chef Michael DeAngelis, who oversees a complete menu of an eclectic mix of American nouvelle cuisine and comfort food with exceptional presentations. Lunch, dinner, and late-night menus are available, and every day a soup and a quesadilla of the day are offered. There's a beautiful banquet area upstairs.

Extras: Open-mike night with karaoke every other Thursday. NFL Sunday Ticket.

Special considerations: Kids welcome. Vegetarian meals available. Handicapped-accessible.

Parking: Street parking or one of many parking garages in the area.

Lodging in the area: Howard Johnson Express Inn, 26 Route 1 North, New Brunswick, 732-828-8000; Hyatt Regency New Brunswick, 2 Albany Street, New Brunswick, 732-873-1234; The Heldrich, 10 Livingston Avenue, New Brunswick, 732-729-4670.

Area attractions: There are three museums of note on the Rutgers campuses. The **Jane Voorhees Zimmerli Art Museum** (71 Hamilton Street, New Brunswick, 732-932-7237) has collections of Soviet underground art and Belgian Art Nouveau posters, classics of illustration. The **New Jersey Museum of Agriculture** (103 College Farm Road, North Brunswick, 732-249-2077) shows the tools and methods used in days gone by, a great chance to display your knowledge (or ignorance) to your kids. The **Rutgers Geology Museum**

(geology.rutgers.edu/museum.shtml), on the second floor of Geology Hall on the main campus, displays a mastodon found in Salem County, dinosaur tracks from Towaco, and an Egyptian mummy.

New Brunswick has its own small theater district on Livingston Avenue. The **George Street Playhouse** (9 Livingston Avenue, 732-846-2895) puts on original and established plays in an intimate setting. The much larger **State Theater** (15 Livingston Avenue, 732-246-7469) is a restored classic that hosts musical acts, dance, and opera. The **Crossroads Theater** (7 Livingston Avenue, 732-545-8100) produces original works and bills itself as "the nation's premiere African American theater."

Other area beer sites: There used to be this thing called a "neighborhood bar," a vanishing breed today. Map in hand, we went looking for these hidden gems in New Brunswick. First we ran into an unusual eatery, **Stuff Yer Face** (49 Easton Avenue, 732-247-1727), which not only majors in stromboli making, but also has a remarkable selection of draft and bottled beers. Any place that has a separate beer menu is my kind of place. You can choose one of the strombolis on the menu or have one prepared "your way" with any of thirty stuffings; then you'll have to choose a beer that complements your selection. They also have a full menu of burgers, salads, pizzas, and sandwiches, all at reasonable prices. In nice weather, you can enjoy your meal on the outside patio. After we wandered back out into the neighborhood, we spied **McCormick's Pub** (266 Somerset Avenue, 732-247-7822), a very small bar with just a few stools and a couple of tables with built-in checker and backgammon boards. The backbar shelf has a small collection of old beer bottles and breweriana that haven't seen a dust rag since they were placed there. But there's some good beer on the twenty taps. Take a moment to look at that bar: More than twenty years' worth of initials, names, dates, and God knows what else are carved into it. Now this is a neighborhood bar! Coming back out of the neighborhood, we stopped at **Old Man Rafferty's** (106 Albany Street, 732-846-6153), which is billed as an Irish bar and restaurant. Decorated in warm earthtones interspersed with wooden accents, it is huge yet bright and cheery. The bar offers the usual suspects on tap, though the bottles hold a surprise or two with a few local offerings.

Just a short walk from here and only a block away from Harvest Moon is the **Old Bay Restaurant** (61–63 Church Street, 732-246-3111). Who would expect to find a French Creole-Cajun restaurant in New Brunswick? Yet in this former bank building, the owners have reproduced a New Orleans experience, from the decor to the authentic menu. If you remember the Old Bay from its glory days as a beer hot spot, one of the premier establishments on the East Coast, stop by again; the beer selection may not be what it once was, but it's quite good. Take the opportunity to raise a glass to the memory of the man who engineered those years of beer excitement, Chris Demetri.

The Bridgewater branch of **The Office** (Route 22 and Thompson Avenue, Bridgewater, 908-469-0066) is typical of the chain.

The best locations for take-home beer are **Buy Rite** (456 Renaissance Boulevard, North Brunswick, 732-951-3822); **Marketplace Wines and Liquors** (647 Route 18 South, East Brunswick, 732-432-9393); and **Super Saver Liquors** (44 West Prospect Street, East Brunswick, 732-238-2022).

J. J. Bitting Brewing Company

33 Main Street, Woodbridge, NJ
732-634-2929
www.njbrewpubs.com

Ever see an old building and envision what its possibilities could be? That's what occurred to Mike Cerami of J. J. Bitting Brewing Company in Woodbridge. This building, constructed circa 1915, was home to the J. J. Bitting Coal and Grain Company until the 1950s, when oil and gas became the fuels of choice and the car the preferred mode of transport. The edifice was once the tallest building in the city and the hub of the downtown area. Trains picked up and delivered to this once-thriving business, replete with its own rail siding. When it was sold, it was subdivided and became a furniture store, appliance retailer, and other businesses until it finally closed in 1962.

Then it sat for thirty-five years and was slated for demolition when Mike realized what he had to do. "I had seen brewpubs in the West," he told me. "I knew I had to come back and open one here. I did not realize at first that they were already legal in New Jersey, so I inquired and then applied right away." The extensive additions and renovations to this beautifully engineered building began in earnest as the papers were shuffled. The post-and-beam construction dates it, and Mike used simple decor that was in keeping with the ambience of this once industrial space.

Walk through the front door, and the brightly polished copper fermenters under glass leave no doubt you're in a brewpub. The original loading dock area is now occupied by tables and chairs. The arched windows were the dock doors, through which many a bag of grain and coal passed. While you sit at your table enjoying the handcrafted brews and fresh food, imagine workers unloading the railcars by hand when long days for low pay were the norm. If only the walls could talk.

Beers brewed: Year-round: Victoria's Golden Ale, JJ's Raspberry Wheat, and Avenel Amber. Seasonals: Bad Boy Oktoberfest (GABF Bronze, 2000), Stout, Porter, Schwarzbier, Dunkel, IPA, Pale Ale, Bitter, Double IPA, Bock, California Common, Irish Red.

The Pick: You know you've got to try the cask beer, whatever it is, and we'll play cagey on the actual Pick too: Get the dark beer. August's good at them; try whatever he's got. You won't be disappointed.

The railroad still runs by the brewpub, but it's an elevated commuter train now. Just across the street is the station, so you can ride the rails and take driving out of the equation when you are planning your visit.

"Our little toy train that circumnavigates the public area pays homage to the railroad history of the community," Mike explained. "Everybody gets a kick out of watching it make its rounds while they enjoy their visit." What a nice touch to a historic place.

Hidden on a small third-floor platform at the top of the atrium is the brewery. It's built up and out of the way so the brewer, August Lightfoot, can ply his trade undisturbed by the general public, but he also must trek up and down the stairs constantly. "It keeps me in shape," he kidded.

True to the building's history, grain is still delivered, though not in the quantities it once was. Of course, horses aren't pulling wagons down Main Street nowadays either. The grain enters as bags of malt and is magically transformed into our favorite beverage.

How does the grain make the trip from the ground floor to those third-floor brewing vessels? Surely August doesn't have to lug it up the stairs, does he? Well, luckily the malt mill is situated in a special room on the ground floor, and the crushed malt is pneumatically transferred from there to the hopper. A great thing, air! (But can you imagine what a broken pipe might do to the space?)

When I asked the brewer why he produces only three flagship beers, he replied, "It allows me to produce more of the beers I want to brew and the ones the customers demand." Three to four seasonals are on tap concurrently, in addition to a cask-conditioned selection on the hand-

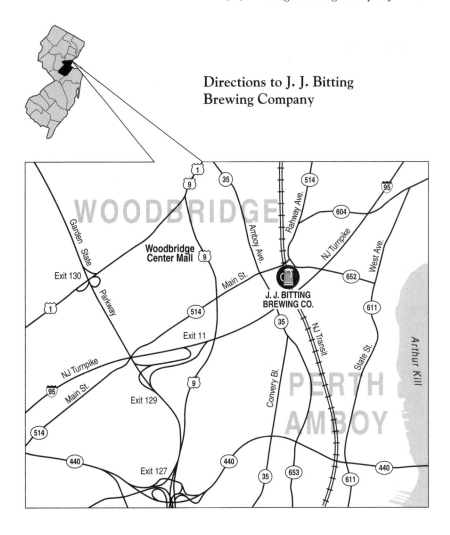

Directions to J. J. Bitting Brewing Company

pump. "I like to keep at least one dark beer and one pale ale pouring all the time, and rotate them through the styles," August said.

What's that I spy on the horizon? Thar she blows! Every third Tuesday of the month there is a WHALES (Woodbridge Homebrewers Ale and Lager Enthusiast Society) sighting at the brewpub. Members of the pod beach themselves for a couple of hours and enjoy tasting the fruits of their labor. Discussions of new methods, ingredients, and equipment are usually on the agenda, and occasionally professional brewers stop by to pass on their wisdom. I have no doubt that recipes of all kinds are traded and reviewed when these aficionados get together. Once a year, Mr. Lightfoot brews a big batch of their Double IPA for a seasonal tap (and a few growlers for the members). The same hops are not always available, so August tweaks the recipe each year by using different species of lupulins.

J. J. Bitting was named the second-best brewpub in America by BeerAdvocate.com in 2003. That was based on overall beer reviews and ratings and was quite a feat for a small place in northern New Jersey.

Want to enjoy the sights and sounds of the city while you dine? There is a rooftop patio just off the second floor that overlooks the downtown area, open only when the weather is pleasant enough to accommodate patrons. From here you can observe the hustle and bustle of the people below yet remain distant from it. Looking back toward the building, you can see the brewing system above you on the next floor of the atrium.

There is also a small dining area on the second floor of the atrium overlooking the bar. Here is a space decorated with painted wall hangings by Jim Tuscano, who also provides the musical entertainment on Thursday nights. This wide-open space is dominated by the sight of the brewery overhead and the echoes from the bar resounding through the area.

Be sure to visit this little piece of Woodbridge history and enjoy what it has to offer for both the diner and the beer enthusiast.

Opened: February 1997.
Owner: Mike Cerami.
Brewer: August Lightfoot.
System: 10-barrel DME system, 700 barrels annual capacity.
Production: 640 barrels in 2006.
Brewpub hours: Monday through Thursday, 11:30 A.M. to 1 A.M.; Friday and Saturday, 11:30 A.M. to 2 A.M.; Sunday, 3 P.M. to 1 A.M.
Tours: Anytime the brewer is available.
Take-out beer: Half-gallon growlers and kegs.
Food: American pub fare. A comprehensive menu that includes American comfort foods, southwestern options, and standard entrées.
Extras: Live music Thursday nights by Jim Tuscano. A full bar is available. Friday nights at 9:30, it's Jazz@J.J.'s, with different artists every week.
Special considerations: Kids welcome. Vegetarian meals available. Handicapped-accessible.
Parking: Street parking and a strip-mall lot across the street.
Lodging in the area: Comfort Suites Woodbridge, 1275 Routes 1 and 9, Avenel, 732-396-3000; Courtyard Edison/Woodbridge, 3105 Woodbridge Avenue, Edison, 732-738-1991; Hampton Inn Woodbridge, 370 Route 9 North, Woodbridge, 732-855-6900.

Area attractions: See entry for Pizzeria Uno.

Other area beer sites: If you're a train buff—and if you're at Bitting, it's a good bet—you'll want to stop in at the **Waiting Room** (66 East Cherry Street, Rahway, 732-815-1042). It's on a quiet side street, about a block from the New Jersey Transit tracks through town, and it's done up to look like an old railroad waiting room: high tin ceiling, open space, and a long bar along the side. The beer's good, the food's exceptional (try the house-made soups), the service is quick and intelligent, even the music is a great eclectic mix. Train buff or not, it's definitely worth a stop. Also see *Pizzeria Uno,* only ten minutes from J. J. Bitting. For take-home, try **Bottle Smart** (489 Route 1 South, Woodbridge, 732-726-0077).

Pizzeria Uno

61 U.S. Highway 1, Metuchen, NJ 08840
732-548-7979
www.unos.com

What goes better with pizza than beer? Why, freshly made beer, of course. The pizza-themed brewpub is mainly a West Coast phenomenon, but here in the Garden State, we are blessed with one such establishment: Pizzeria Uno in Metuchen is the sole location in this chain of more than two hundred restaurants where they brew their own beer. The company was hoping to have a chain of brewpubs to supply all their locations with beer, but because of the restrictive laws in some states, they found it not in their best interest to proceed further than this single venue. A loss for the nation, but a win for New Jersey.

Just off I-287 on U.S. Route 1, and easily accessible from the Garden State Parkway and New Jersey Turnpike, this restaurant is situated near the industrial park complex in Edison and surrounded by the area's largest shopping malls. The locale gives it a built-in customer base, but the name and reputation will draw patrons in only once. To keep the people returning, you have to be good, and this

Beers brewed: Year-round: Bootlegger Blonde Ale, Station House Red Ale, 32 Inning Ale, Ike's IPA, Gust n' Gale Porter. Seasonals: ESB, Weizenbock, Wee Heavy, Oatmeal Stout, Milk Stout, Hefeweizen, Oktoberfest, Dark Mild, Wit, Blonde Bock.

place has proven itself. Since the opening in March 1998, a large number of customers stop by regularly to be treated to the extensive menu and some of the best beer in the area.

Brewer Mike Sella, who has been on-premises since the venue opened, brews five beers in the flagship line, but he really keeps the customers coming in with a wide array of seasonals. For first-time visitors (or those who enjoy variety), a sampler of all the current beers is always available to familiarize them with the different styles. All you cask ale fans take note: Every Friday, Mike puts a pin (5-gallon cask) of one of his beers up on the bar and pours it until it's gone, usually in just a few hours. Arrive early to be sure to get your share.

Recently the restaurant added growler sales to the repertoire. When you find which one of Mike's creations hits your fancy, you can take home a half-gallon of fresh beer for all to enjoy. Bring back the growler and refill it every time you visit. This allows Mike to empty his tanks more quickly and gives him a chance to venture into different styles to keep the tanks full and the beer geeks interested. It also keeps him very busy.

Pizzeria Uno is obviously geared toward pizza and Italian food, but a full range of culinary styles is served, both in the elaborately decorated dining room and for take-out. Soups, salads, wraps, sandwiches, pasta, steaks, seafood . . . you name it, it's on the multipage menu. Just to peruse this extensive menu will take a while, so you might start out by ordering your favorite appetizers and libations to allow you time to choose your entrée. In addition to the handcrafted beers, the restaurant offers a full bar with all your favorite spirits, as well as a nice selection of wines. Even some of the megabrewers' bottles are available.

The dining room is a large, comfortable space with tables and oversize booths. Six people can be seated in the booths with room to spare. Tiffany-style lamps light each table, and TVs are scattered about the area. Everywhere you look around you, there is something different. Memorabilia and paraphernalia of all kinds cover much of the walls here . . . baseball, movies, license plates, and so on. There is also a separate dining area that can be used for parties and special events. Beer dinners are held here several times a year, with special menus and beer offerings.

In the big, rectangular bar area, you are never out of viewing range of the dozen or so TVs that keep you up-to-date on all the sports, news, and financial happenings. During football season, Uno's offers the NFL Ticket on Sundays, letting you relax and choose from a multitude of

The Pick: My choice is the Dark Mild, a nicely brewed low-alcohol session beer with lots of flavor. Sometimes that's all you need, and you might just want to have more than one.

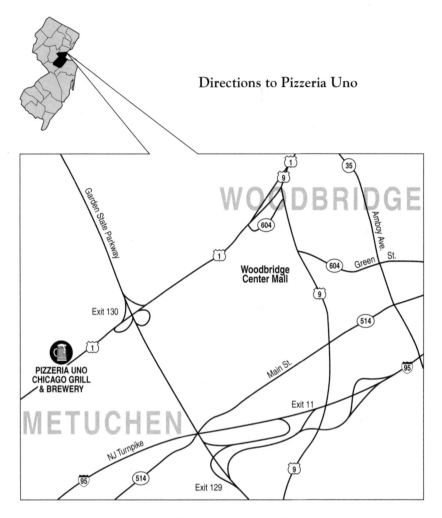

Directions to Pizzeria Uno

games that can be displayed simultaneously. No need to contend with cold, snowy, or rainy weather to see your favorite teams play every week; just stop in, find a good seat, grab a beer, and enjoy.

But the real show is in the small glass-encased room adjoining the bar—the brewery. Here Mike performs the magic that is called fermentation, blending the water, grain, hops, and yeast into the nectar we refer to as beer. If you can catch Mike in one of his rare idle moments, ask him to explain how he performs these feats. Understanding the process certainly imparts a better appreciation for the brewer's efforts.

Opened: March 1998.
Owner: Uno Restaurant Corporation.

Brewer: Mike Sella.

System: 15-barrel Pub Brewing system.

Production: 650 barrels in 2006.

Brewpub hours: Weekends, 11:30 A.M. to 1 A.M.; weekdays, 11:30 A.M. to midnight.

Tours: On request, when brewer is available.

Take-out beer: Half-gallon growlers.

Food: As you'd expect, pizzas of all kinds are offered: thin crust or Chicago Deep Dish, with a long list of toppings. You're not always in that mood, so they also have a variety of salads, burgers, steaks, seafood, and desserts.

Extras: Karaoke on Thursdays. Cask beer tapped on Friday nights. NFL Ticket on Sundays (in season).

Special considerations: Kids welcome. Vegetarian meals available; lots of pastas, salads, and pizzas. Handicapped-accessible.

Parking: Free parking on large lot.

Lodging in the area: Hilton Garden Inn, 50 Raritan Center Parkway, Edison, 732-225-0900; Comfort Inn Edison, 831 Route 1 South, Edison, 732-287-0171; Red Roof Inn, 860 New Durham Road, Edison, 732-248-9326.

Area attractions: You're in Edison country; this is where America's most driven inventor developed the practical lightbulb, sound recordings, motion pictures, and an amazing number of patented inventions. The ***Thomas Alva Edison Memorial Tower and Museum*** (37 Christie Street, Edison, 732-549-3299, www.menloparkmuseum.com) is packed with Edison memorabilia, photos, and sound recordings. The tower is a monument to the man, topped with a giant lightbulb.

Other area beer sites: The ***Fox and Hound English Pub and Grille*** (250 Menlo Park Drive, Edison), an outpost of the chain of pubs, serves up some variety in an atmosphere that is fairly similar to an analogous British pub. Otherwise, well, Harvest Moon and J. J. Bitting aren't far away.

Trap Rock Restaurant and Brewery

279 Springfield Avenue, Berkeley Heights, NJ 07922
908-665-1755
www.traprockrestaurant.net

Gourmet food and good beer? That was an unheard-of combination when Trap Rock Restaurant and Brewery opened up back in 1997 in this small Union County community. It was a new concept in dining that is just now coming into its own more than ten years later. This highly acclaimed venue has passed the test of time and has delighted connoisseurs with its innovative culinary insights ever since.

Prior to Trap Rock, the building had been home to several different restaurants, but when Harvest Restaurants bought it, they decided to add a brewery and make it a bit more upscale than what was normally considered a brewpub.

The building was extensively renovated to emulate a European Alpine ski lodge and is a stunning piece of architecture. Never having been skiing, I could only imagine that the Garden Room would be the epitome of the Aspen après ski retreat. A high vaulted ceiling, a large stone fireplace, and tall windows with a view accompany the intimate table settings to allow you to kick back and enjoy the experience. The Brewers Room is an equally appointed space but is hidden away upstairs for a truly private setting. Both are available for parties or banquets.

When Trap Rock first opened, the cuisine they offered was exceptional, dominated by French-influenced selections, and the service was impeccable. But to grow with the times, a more eclectic menu has been initiated in the last couple of years to attract those just dropping in for a snack or a quick lunch.

"We have a loyal corporate lunch crowd but depend on the locals for our weeknights and weekends. I believed we needed to appeal to a wider audience, being where we are," explained Charlie

Beers brewed: Year-round: Ghost Pony Helles Lager (GABF Bronze, 2001), Hathor Red Lager, Kestrel IPA, Six Witches Stout, JP Pilsner. Seasonals: Melisbock, Simon Session Ale, Octoberfest, Maibock, Roggenbock, Pale Ale, Belgian Blonde Ale, Hefeweizen, Razzywheat, Porter, Colonial Porter, Pumpkin Ale, Imperial Stout, Barleywine.

Schroeder, the brewer for the last five years, "so we began to offer more comfort foods and a little less haute cuisine." Still prepared with quality as a priority, the offerings remain exquisite yet familiar and the service is flawless. The ambience was intentionally given a highbrow feel so as to cater to the upscale customer.

The Pick: My first choice from the regular lineup would be the Hathor Red, a nicely malted German-style Märzen with a slight hint of noble hops.

To showcase the pairing of food and brew, beer dinners are held usually three times a year: spring, summer, and fall. The seasonal offerings of both food and beer are matched up to provide a culinary delight for the attendees.

Besides the on-premises handcrafted beer, an impressive list of international and domestic wines is available to satisfy any oenophile. In addition, for those like myself who enjoy a wee dram after dinner, a nice selection of single-malt scotches is lined up coincidentally on the "top shelf" of the bar.

Trap Rock was the parent company's first foray into the restaurant world. Since then, five other locations have been added to the repertoire. The six restaurants couldn't be more different. Each one has its own "hook" and target clientele: rustic Italian, nouveau American, steak and seafood, and light elegance. The tie that binds is the "wine factor." Each place offers an extensive assortment of wines that fit the food style. Trap Rock beer, contract-brewed by High Point Brewing, is also offered in several of the locations.

Charlie is the consummate brewpub brewer: He loves what he does and enjoys dealing with people. Trained at the Siebel Institute and American Brewers Guild, he apprenticed here in New Jersey. After trying to find his niche working for several production breweries, he was offered the chance to take over the kettles at Trap Rock in 2002.

Why would you leave a good job at a large brewery for a brewpub? "First, I was commuting every day to Pennsylvania from New Jersey," he explained. "This position would put me close to home. Second, the opportunity to run your own brewery and be able to sit and watch the people enjoy the fruits of your labor right there is so rewarding. Brewing is an art and the consumers are the critics. I love to talk to them and get feedback about what I'm doing or should be doing."

From time to time, someone requests that Charlie brew a certain style. He'll look into working it into the schedule if he feels that demand warrants its production. There are just some things he cannot do and still keep the beer flowing in all the taps. Mr. S. usually tends the tun himself,

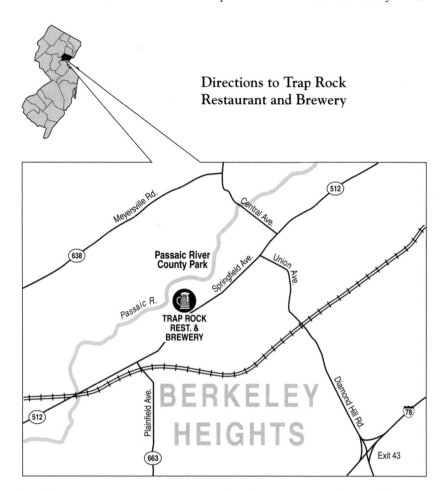

Directions to Trap Rock Restaurant and Brewery

but from time to time when a specialty beer is requested, he allows the petitioner in to assist. What a thrill that must be for a homebrewer.

The name Trap Rock interested me, and I queried Charlie about its roots. "There are local quarries mining 'trap rock,' which is used in the production of concrete and macadam," he explained. "Some of these sites are still in operation, but not to the extent they used to be. These minerals are coveted by collectors and may still be procured at several locations nearby."

Grab your rock-collecting gear and pack your best duds, and head to Berkeley Heights to enjoy the experiences this area offers.

Opened: April 1997.
Owner: Harvest Restaurants, Inc.

Brewer: Charles Schroeder.

System: 7-barrel DME system, 500 barrels annual capacity.

Production: 425 barrels in 2006.

Brewpub hours: Monday through Wednesday, 11:30 A.M. to 10 P.M.; Thursday and Friday, 11:30 A.M. to 11 P.M.; Saturday, 4 P.M. to 11 P.M.; and Sunday, 4 P.M. to 9 P.M.

Tours: By appointment.

Take-out beer: Half-gallon growlers and kegs.

Food: Nouvelle American cuisine with an accent on updated comfort foods and fusion seafood dishes. Dinner reservations are recommended.

Extras: A full-service bar with an extensive assortment of wines, scotches, and the brewpub's handcrafted beers. Always something on the handpump.

Special considerations: Trap Rock is not really a kids' kind of place. Vegetarian meals available. Handicapped-accessible.

Parking: Limited parking on-premises and in neighboring lot at night. Valet parking on weekends.

Lodging in the area: Best Western Murray Hill, 535 Central Avenue, New Providence, 908-665-9200; Grand Summit Hotel, 520 Springfield Avenue, Summit, 800-457-4000; Howard Johnson Express, 1011 Route 22 West, North Plainfield, 908-753-6500.

Area attractions: The *Visual Arts Center* (68 Elm Street, Summit, 908-273-9121) is a nonprofit organization whose mission it is to bring art to the masses through exhibits, lectures, seminars, and classes. Why not help them out with that? *Watchung Reservation* (452 New Providence Road, Mountainside, 908-789-3670) is a Union County park with more than 2,000 acres for outdoor activities such as camping, hiking, and biking. You can play golf at *Summit Golf Course* (189 River Road, Summit, 908-277-6828) or *Warrenbrook Golf Course* (500 Warrenville Road, Warren, 908-754-8402).

Other area beer sites: I have not had much luck finding good beer selections at fancy hotel bars. They tend to serve a transient crowd that's mostly interested in having a no-risk drinking experience. Happily, things are quite different at the *Tap Room at Somerset Hills Hotel* (200 Liberty Corner Road, Warren, 908-647-6700). Not only are there good taps, but they are being actively marketed with flyers on the bar that note a rotating IPA tap, a regional and international craft beer of the month, and a bottled seasonal of the month. There are also dedicated taps for Ommegang, Brooklyn, and Cricket Hill American Lager. Maybe the nicest touch is the offer of "flights" of beer and wine samples—three small glasses of different drinks for the guest who wants to sample before settling on a full glass. All this, and a comfortable lounge? Book me a room! At first the **Stirling Hotel** (227 Main Street, Stirling, 908-649-6919) looked like just another rough-and-ready place, cluttered with the accumulated decorative debris of decades, albeit with some excellent and uncommon taps and a pretty laid-back beer-informed staff. But then one of them suggested I take a look out back. There's a *lot* going on here: a couple of outdoor bars that run through the warmer months and into the fall, a small park, room for classic car shows, and a nice dining deck. The menu's solid and not wholly conventional—variety is good at the Stirling Hotel.

There are three **Office** locations within 8 miles of Trap Rock: at 61 Union Place, across from the train station in Summit (908-522-0550); 3 South Avenue West in Cranford (908-272-3888); and 3 South Street in Morristown (973-285-0220).

For six-packs to go, try **Berkeley Wine Company** (500 Springfield Avenue, Berkeley Heights, 908-464-3610); **Total Wine and More** (950 Springfield Road, Union, 908-688-2453); **Stirling Fine Wines** (1168 Valley Road, Stirling, 908-647-5580); **Gary's Wine and Marketplace** (121 Main Street, Madison, 973-822-0200); or **Whole Foods Market** (222 Main Street, Madison, 973-822-8444).

Micros, Brewpubs, and Craft Brewers

Much of what people say is said because they don't want to say something more blunt or honest. Code words, euphemisms, and evasions are part of our everyday speech. Here's a little secret of the beer world: *Microbrewery* and *craft brewery* are just more code words.

When the new brewing movement started in America in the 1970s, no one knew what to call these little breweries. "Brewery pub," "boutique brewery," and "microbrewery" were all used. By the early 1980s, two words had settled into general use: "microbrewery" and "brewpub." (We're glad "boutique brewery" fell out of the running.) At the time, industry pundits defined a brewpub as a brewery that sold most of its beer in an in-house taproom. They defined a microbrewery as a brewery that produced less than 15,000 barrels a year. These terms gained legal recognition in some states, as deals were struck to allow the new businesses to start up and as tax rates were determined. The federal government acknowledged the special nature of small breweries in the early 1990s, granting a substantial tax break to those with an annual production under 50,000 barrels.

Eventually the industry itself came up with a whole set of labels. "Brewpub" continued to be used for breweries that sold the large majority of their beer on-premises by the glass. "Microbrewery" was for packaging breweries whose production was less than 50,000 barrels. "Regional" breweries applied to smaller ones established before 1970 that did not distribute to all of America, such as Yuengling. Nationally distributing giants like Anheuser-Busch, Miller, Coors, and Pabst were dubbed "national brewers" or "megabrewers."

But the growth of some successful microbreweries has made even 50,000 barrels an uncomfortable fit. Boston Beer Company, the contract brewery responsible for the Samuel Adams line of beers, sells over a million barrels a year, and Sierra Nevada Brewing Company, an early microbrewery that produces all its own beer, is pushing 700,000 barrels. Clearly these are no longer microbreweries, yet their beer is exactly the same as it was. To be called a microbrewery has a cachet to it that most microbrewers don't want to surrender. What to call them?

Some propose the blanket term "craft brewery." This implies that the beer is somehow crafted, rather than produced in a factory. Craft breweries are different, the explanation goes, because the beer is made in single batches, not in several that are then combined in one huge tank or blended after fermentation to ensure consistency. Well, no, because a lot of these brewers do blend. And they have automated brewhouses, they have malt silos instead of using bagged malt, some of them pasteurize their beer, and the big ones do look pretty much like beer factories.

New Jersey's laws actually put more of a straitjacket on brewery definitions than most states' laws do. In New Jersey, a brewpub is a brewpub, period. You can't bottle in a brewpub for sale to a wholesaler, for example, and off-premises sales are limited to growlers. Conversely, breweries are not allowed to have a pub, nor can the same company own one of each. The reasoning is supposedly to keep giants like Anheuser-Busch from opening little breweries everywhere, something A-B has not shown any evidence of wanting to do in other, more open states.

The fact is, "microbrewery" has always been a code word, and so has "craft brewery." They both mean the same thing. They describe a brewery that makes beer in an authentic manner—using ingredients and techniques appropriate to a given style of beer or brewing—and that brews beers other than mainstream American-style lager. What should these businesses be called? How about *breweries?*

The distinctions are really all nonsense. Brewery size has nothing to do with the quality of a beer. Guinness Stout, the beer to which most microbrewers hopefully compare their own dry stouts, is brewed by a globe-girdling gargantuan of a company.

In this book, we have bowed to convention and used the words "brewpub," "microbrewery," and "craft brewery." "Brewpub" is the best of these terms. A brewery where beer is taken directly from the conditioning tanks to serving tanks and sold from a tap on-premises truly deserves a unique name.

But why not simply call all the others breweries? To differentiate a brewery based on the kind of beer it makes seems to be missing the point. Categorizing them by size penalizes the ones that succeed and outgrow the class. Call them breweries, and then let the beer do the talking.

Down the Shore

A h-h-h, the Jersey Shore! More than 100 miles of coastline on the mighty Atlantic Ocean, with some of the most beautiful beaches on the East Coast. For many, it means family vacations that have been spent at the shore in family homes passed down through generations . . . sun and fun on the beach, nights on the boardwalks enjoying the games and rides, and even a favorite bar with some great local bands playing. For others, it means an escape from the heat and hubbub of the city and a place to just sit and enjoy a good book while lazing on the beach or front porch. Maybe you even met your significant other during one of those summers, and now you're bringing your family down to enjoy the sights and sounds. No matter what the reason, the Jersey Shore has been *the* place to visit for more than a century.

The beaches from Cape May to Sandy Hook have been a destination for New Yorkers and Pennsylvanians for as long as one can remember. Hopping on the Garden State Parkway or the Atlantic City Expressway has made the trip a simple one. The Parkway runs the length of the state close to the shore and has been the main artery for shoregoers since 1952. The Atlantic City Expressway is fairly new in comparison, built to accommodate the Philadelphia summer exodus to the shore communities.

Many of the towns are "summer towns," with transient populations that swell in the summer and shrink in the winter. A lot of the businesses are seasonal as well and must follow the ebb and flow of the "shoobies" and board up in the winter, as the local populations are not enough to sustain them.

In the southern part of the state, that trend has seen a slight reversal since the inception of casino gambling in Atlantic City. The large numbers of casino employees have taken up residence close to work,

53

and the proliferation of housing developments has led to a population explosion in the surrounding communities.

But this is not unique to Atlantic City anymore. Urban sprawl has made some of the resorts closer to the New York metro area more affluent bedroom communities with a large commuter demographic. Opulent houses have been built on the beachfront in high densities to maximize profits of the developers. This has had the unexpected result of privatizing some of the beach areas, which has been a bone of contention for visitors and residents alike. The courts have usually sided with the petitioners who seek access, but compromises on rectification continue.

Years ago, the bar scene at these shore destinations was alive and kicking. Thousands of young people would converge on these resorts in the summer to enjoy the music and the libations these venues had to offer. The hundreds of bars that used to populate these towns have now dwindled to a handful. Aggressive enforcement of stricter drunk-driving laws is some of the reason, as well as redevelopment of large urban areas. Condos and business offices are much more lucrative ventures than taverns. The neighborhood bar does not exist in many places anymore.

In our younger days, we could listen to bands on every block in Atlantic City. Places like the Lemon Tree, Club Harlem, and the Wonder Gardens brought in thousands of people to have a drink and be entertained by top-flight performers. Margate and Somers Point catered to the younger crowd also, with bars like the White House, Gables, Maloney's, Tony Mart's, Mother's, and Bayshores. And who could forget the Dunes—three bars open all night, with music in all three! Now you'd be hard-pressed to find many bars with live music outside the casinos.

Up north, a similar situation exists. Once a vibrant resort, Asbury Park has seen a decrease in visitors and the closing of many of its most famous landmarks: the amusement piers on its Boardwalk, theaters, and its downtown area. Happily, the famous Stone Pony is still one of the solid venues in the city. Considered home to the rock greats Bruce Springsteen, Jon Bon Jovi, and Southside Johnny, it is still in full tilt today, with acts appearing year-round on its stage. The area is now in a state of revitalization in hopes of bringing back part of those "glory days."

Places like Seaside Heights, Ocean City, and Wildwood are still going strong. Their boardwalks are home to several amusement piers and water parks. Families flock to these resorts by the thousands to enjoy their family-oriented attractions and year-round events.

Revitalization is a modern-day watchword. So many of the resorts never kept up with the times and paid the price when the sociological revolution occurred . . . the baby boomers grew up! The advent of the two-income household and the seemingly endless parade of chores that need to be done have kept many families from finding the time to use the family summer homes. Some were sold, some rented, others just left in disrepair, bringing about a decline in the once vibrant neighborhoods.

But there are so many success stories today in reversing this problem. The city of Red Bank is one case in point. It has revitalized by bringing in new businesses and residents to maintain its growth. Theaters and art galleries have sprung up throughout the area, and redevelopment of the downtown neighborhood has attracted more people to the businesses that have opened.

Atlantic City, for years the "Playground of the World," found this out the hard way. The cancer that took over this once thriving city was in its final stages, and death was imminent. For better or worse, the casinos saved my hometown from becoming a Newark or Camden, which themselves are now in the midst of a recovery. Much of the Jersey Shore will never see the glorious times that used to be, but everything must adapt to the new era, and resorts are no different. This new generation is not so thrilled with the simple pleasures we enjoyed, and new modes of entertainment must be devised to accommodate.

Atlantic City is undergoing a beer revitalization as well. Good beer is creeping in slowly, as more distributors carry craft products and the drinking public demands better selection. In addition, several guys from Harrah's—Mark Monte, Bert Bertino, Jon Henderson, and Jerome Robinson—have singlehandedly changed the face of the beer market in the area with the advent of the now annual Atlantic City Beer Festival held in March.

The only real beer festival that existed in the state prior to this was the Garden State Craft Brewers Guild Festival. The New Jersey Department of Alcoholic Beverage Control (ABC) had no guidelines by which to govern an event like this, but the AC Fest forced it to confront the questions asked by the show producers. Now, at least, if you want to organize a festival, you know what criteria you must meet. The overwhelming success of this two-day event has exposed many of the locals to a new world of beer they never knew existed.

The eastern coast of New Jersey is also home to many wildlife preserves, bird sanctuaries, and state parks. The Edwin B. Forsythe National Wildlife Refuge has two locations on the coast, one in Brigantine and the other in Barnegat. Here many species of wetland animals are protected from possible extinction by the impinging development of their habitats. Cape May Point State Park, Corson's Inlet State Park, Barnegat Lighthouse State Park, Island Beach State Park, and Gateway National Recreation Area are among those that dot the barrier islands. Visitors can enjoy the many recreational facilities these parks afford: nature trails and programs, swimming, surfing, fishing, and many other activities. Bring the family for a day of fun and education.

Not far from Long Beach Island, on the Mullica River, is the Wharton State Forest, 115,000 acres of preserved woodlands with activities of all kinds. There are miles of trails for mountain biking, horseback riding, and hiking; rivers, lakes, and streams for swimming and canoeing; campsites for tents and trailers; cabins for noncampers to stay in; and the colonial village of Batsto for a history lesson.

Of course, you can enjoy some of these activities without having to go to the parks. Fishing, for example, is one of the most popular attractions all along the coast. You can rent a boat for the day along the inland waterway, take one of the many excursion trips out into the ocean, or just surf-fish from a beach.

Swimming is allowed at any number of places. Protected beaches— that is, a public beach where lifeguards are employed to see to your safety—are recommended. Nowadays, not all the beaches are free, and some towns require the purchase of tags to help defray the cost of maintaining the services. Be sure to check on the rules of your destination so your vacation won't be ruined by an unexpected problem.

Hop off anywhere along the parkway, go east, and you're at the Jersey Shore, but the cities you pass through to get to the beaches also have lots to offer and might be worth a stopover. For one, lodging prices are usually a lot lower. For those on a tight budget, you might consider that short trip to the beach worth the money saved. Seasonal businesses must make enough money in that short season to last all year, so prices are normally higher in the beach towns than on the mainland.

In Toms River, on the way to Seaside Heights, you can find a multitude of shopping malls and restaurants, as well as hotels and even good beer bars. A little farther south, close to Barnegat, lies the small town of Waretown, whose claim to fame in the region is the Albert Music Hall, the local center for country and bluegrass music. Every Saturday night, aficionados arrive to enjoy the scheduled entertainers.

Back up north, not far from the beach, is one of the last remaining active horse-racing venues in New Jersey. Monmouth Race Track has been a fixture there since 1946 and has live racing and simulcasting in season. Just a ways west of there is the oldest racetrack in the state, Freehold Raceway. Dating back to the nineteenth century, this track still has a long live racing season every year.

See, who says you have to go to the beach or a boardwalk? There is such a variety of activities in this part of the state. We've tried to do some of the beerhunting for you, but small towns hold a lot of secrets. Go out and explore on your own, and see what gems you come up with. Happy beerhunting!

The Original Basil T's Brewery and Italian Grill

183 Riverside Drive, Red Bank, NJ 07701
732-842-5990
www.basilt.com

Basil T's

When Victor Rallo Sr. opened up the Basil T Leaf Restaurant in Red Bank in 1986, I don't believe he ever imagined that his son, Victor Jr., would add a brewery ten years later and take the establishment to a whole new level.

Victor Jr. was always looking for new opportunities and likes to be a trendsetter. "We wanted to make a change, have something different from anyone else," he said. In the early days of brewpubs in the Garden State, there wasn't much information to be had on how successful they could be. There were many nationwide that were opening and closing all in the same year.

Making an investment of that magnitude could not be taken lightly by any competent business-man, but Victor was adamant and proceeded to implement his plan. He knew that the restaurant was working; how could a brewery do anything but enhance the business?

"The brewpub business in general is not good. The only ones that make it are those that serve good food," Victor explained. "That is why we pay a lot of attention to the cuisine. It has paid off for us. Our growth has been 15 percent per year."

Beers brewed: Year-round: Ms. Lucy's Weimaraner Wheat, Rosie's Tale Waggin' Pale Ale, Basil's Rocket Red Ale, Maxwell's Dry Stout (GABF Gold, 2002, 2006; GABF Bronze, 2003). Seasonals: XXX Summer Ale, IPA, Pumpkin Ale, Spiced Apple Wheat, Porter, German Ale, Beer of the Dragon, Big Brown Biere, Imperial Stout.

His business motto has always been "fresh is best." He buys the freshest vegetables, meats, and seafood and makes his own pasta, sauces, and mozzarella cheese; why not fresh beer too? I'm sure that if making his own wine were legal, he'd have his help in the back stomping grapes.

Italians are known not for their love of beer, but for their passion for wine. For that reason, an extensive wine cellar has always been an integral part of their inventory. The traditionalists must be sated.

The Pick: Logically, the multi-award-winning Maxwell's Dry Stout is the obvious choice. It's a full-bodied brew with lots of roast, chocolate, and a very pronounced coffee dryness. The Pale Ale pulls in close behind for me, a perfectly balanced ale that epitomizes what the style should be.

But the beer is the real star here. As you walk up to the building from the parking lot, the first thing you see is the brewery in the front window. You can't imagine how anyone but an elf could ever work in such a confined space. Brewer Gretchen Schmidhausler confirmed that it takes some getting used to, but once you're familiar with the system, it works. The biggest problem with small systems is that brewers are limited in the variety of styles they can brew. They become victims of their own success, which seems to be the mantra of most brewpub brewers.

Keeping up with demand is another common problem. The number of fermenters decides for them how often they can brew. The more popular seasonals sometimes run out quicker than anticipated, and they're left with a void in the tap lines. Gretchen said, "I'm pretty close to the capacity I can brew with this system. Planning is so important in keeping the beer flowing and the customers happy." Of course, there is only so much one person can accomplish in a day.

Gretchen has been a professional brewer for eleven years and brewed at this location since 2001. She is one of the few full-time women brewers in the state. As a matter of fact, there are not that many nationwide. Not that gender has anything to do with the ability to brew great beer, of course.

We have largely forgotten that in earlier times, women were charged with making beer for the family, and with luck had a little left to sell to the neighbors to pay for the next batch. Even though more of the fairer sex are entering the professional arena, they have a long way to go to catch up to the men in numbers.

"There are more women brewers than you think," Gretchen said. "You just don't hear about them. I recently brewed my thousandth batch with Teri Fahrendorf, late of Steelhead Brewing in Oregon, who is on the road to guest brew at breweries all over the U.S. She is looking to sign up other brewsters [women brewers] for the Pink Boots Society."

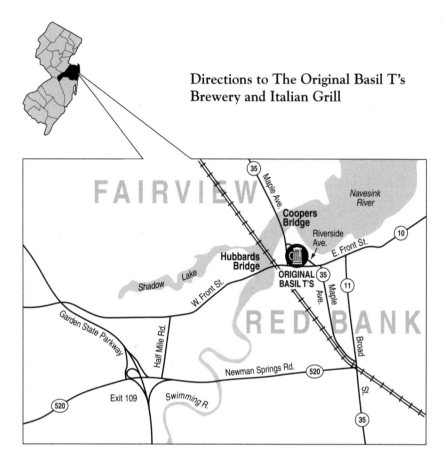

Directions to The Original Basil T's Brewery and Italian Grill

Every year, Gretchen packs up samples of her beer and ships them to Denver for judging at the GABF. Her Maxwell's Dry Stout has won three medals—two golds and a bronze, in two different categories. I was there when she won in 2002 and 2003, and she was practically floating on air after the ceremony. What a fulfilling experience it must be to be chosen the best by your peers out of so many entries.

Gretchen has gathered a very large group of loyal consumers under her beer banner. You can sit at the bar and watch the parade of patrons that come in for a beer and one of the excellent Italian specialties. And what's that hanging from the top of the bar, mugs with numbers on the bottom? Must be a Mug Club.

Believe it or not, Basil T's Mug Club boasts thirteen hundred members. While some places can't even get one off the ground, this small location sells out its subscription every year. For a $24 annual fee, you receive a custom-made 20-ounce ceramic mug, and with each visit, you can fill it with your favorite brew for $3.75. At the end of the year, you take your mug home and fill it with the beer you bring home in your growler or . . . anything. Such a deal!

Speaking of deals, stop in from 4 P.M. to 6 P.M. on weekdays and enjoy a complimentary buffet and happy hour pints for $1 off. This food and Gretchen's beer: It just doesn't get any better than this.

Convenient to the Garden State Parkway, Red Bank is a community on the rise with lots of artsy, highbrow places to visit—art galleries, theaters, restaurants of all kinds. Beer is the redheaded stepdaughter, it seems, as good wine lists are the norm and even mention of mainstream beers is rare. At Basil T's, though, you can have it all: good food, good beer, good wine, and good service. Buon appetito!

Opened: September 1996.

Owner: Victor Rallo Jr.

Brewer: Gretchen Schmidhausler.

System: 7-barrel Pub Brewing system, approximately 700 barrels annual capacity.

Production: 680 barrels in 2006.

Brewpub hours: Open Monday through Saturday, 11 A.M. to 11 P.M.; Sunday, 4 P.M. to 10 P.M.

Tours: If someone is available; ask your server.

Take-out beer: Deluxe growlers.

Food: Traditional gourmet Italian. A solid selection of salads, antipastos, paninis, pizzas, homemade pasta, seafood and meat entrées, not to mention the made-on-premises desserts.

Extras: Full bar. Mug Club. An exquisite wine cellar with some outstanding selections. Live music on Thursday, Friday, and Saturday. Happy hour.

Special considerations: Kids welcome. Vegetarian meals available. Handicapped-accessible.

Parking: On-premises lot.

Lodging in the area: Molly Pitcher Inn, 88 Riverside Drive, Red Bank, 800-221-1372; Oyster Point Hotel, 146 Bodman Place, Red Bank, 800-345-3484; Courtyard by Marriott, 245 Half Mile Road, Red Bank, 732-530-5552.

Area attractions: *Two Rivers Theater* (21 Bridge Avenue, Red Bank, 732-345-1400, www.trtc.org) is a local theater troupe with a multitude of productions during the year. The *Count Basie Theatre* (99 Monmouth Street, Red Bank, 732-842-9000, www.countbasie theatre.org) is a classic theater, built in 1926 and still going strong, with some big-name acts coming through on a regular basis: music, drama, comedians.

Other area beer sites: Victor recently opened a restaurant in nearby Rumson called **Undici.** It's an authentic Tuscan restaurant with New Jersey's largest Italian wine list . . . 350 labels! There's not much around for beer, though. So grab some take-home bottles: Try **Spirits Unlimited** (56 Newman Springs Road, Red Bank, 732-747-4053); **Crates Beverages** (14 North Bridge Street, Red Bank, 732-747-1485); **Bottle King** (1050 Route 35, Middletown, 732-615-2400); or **Ocean Wine and Spirits** (1104 Route 35 South, Ocean Township, 732-660-6700).

Basil T's Brewpub and Italian Grill

1171 Hooper Avenue, Toms River, NJ 08753
732-244-7566
www.basilts.com

Basil T's

What do you do when you've opened a successful brewpub and the concept works so well? Why, open up a second location, of course! Victor Rallo Jr. and staff did just that. After a year of rave reviews at their Red Bank locale, a friend mentioned that the Toms River area was ripe for a brewpub that served the class of cuisine Basil T's was known for. Though Victor at first was hesitant, it only took him several months to find the right location, obtain a few investors, and begin the opening process.

The restaurant is decorated to simulate what I would suppose is a Mediterranean villa. I don't know about you, but I would be very surprised to find a stainless steel brewing system as the centerpiece in my villa. Never having been to that part of the world, I can only guess that they're few and far between. Throughout the building, the mural masterpieces of local artist Gregg Hinlicky pervade the space and set the mood.

It didn't stay Victor's for long, however. "We thought it would be a good move to have a second brewpub in the area, but Toms River never seemed to click for us, so we decided to sell it," Victor explained.

It was bought in 2002 by Peter and Pete Greg-orakis, who made minimal changes. "We always wanted to buy a restaurant together, but something happened that derailed our plans every time," Pete said. "This time everything fell into place, and we found ourselves as owners of Basil T's. We thought about removing the brewery, but we would have to destroy much of the building to accomplish that task."

What to do? Let an expensive system sit idle? That did happen occasionally, while a revolving cast of part-time brewers tended to the system for several years, but once the owners decided to keep it brewing, the search began to find a great brewer to take over the kettles.

Enter Dave Hoffmann. He had helped them procure the previous brewer, who needed to take a personal leave, and Dave figured he'd take over for a while in the interim. An iconic figure in his own right (see Climax Brewing), Dave soon took to this second gig. "I'm having a great time brewing at this location. At Climax, I make the same beers day in and day out. Here I get to play! I've made some styles I've always wanted to brew."

How long will he stay at Basil's? "Once it gets to be a grind and I don't enjoy it anymore, I'll give it up to someone else," he told me. "Other than that, as long as they want me to stay, I'll be here."

The two brothers have nothing but praise for Dave and the job he's doing for them: "Dave has done wonders for the beer here. He has brought it consistency and quality. We hope he stays with us for a long time!"

Now, Dave is a traditional English-German-style brewer, and this is a traditional Mediterranean-style restaurant. Blasphemy, you say? Don't knock it until you've tried it! The clean, crisp styles definitely measure up to the eclectic cuisine served at Basil T's. Ask Dave, he'll tell you. Really, stop in and give it a try for yourself. Maybe your sig-nificant other isn't a beer lover; not a problem. They stock a complete bar and have an extensive wine selection. What Italian restaurant worth its pasta doesn't?

Under the able direction of master chef Steven Farley, the kitchen puts out some of the finest Italian and Mediterranean cuisine anywhere. (His German fare at Oktoberfest time is not so bad either!) "I really don't like to pigeonhole our cuisine here. Sure we make a lot of Mediter-

Beers brewed: Year-round: Barnegat Light, Pale Ale, Toms River Red, Porter. Seasonals: Oktoberfest, Stout Porter, Dop-pel Bock Lager, Nut Brown, Maibock, Helles, Hefeweizen, Pilsener, English Ale, Bavarian Dark Lager, Pumpkin Ale, Win-ter Ale.

The Pick: I have to pick one of Dave's lagers here, after going with an ale at Climax. The Helles is a beauty, proving Hoffmann's touch at getting the most out of his malt.

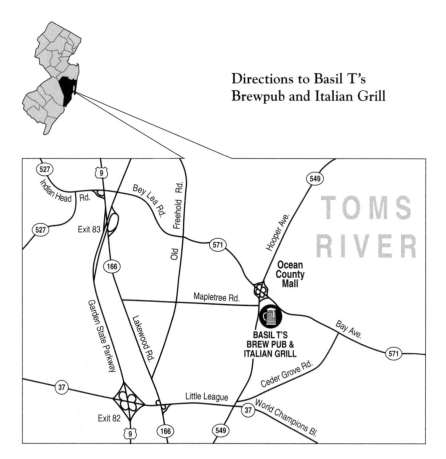

**Directions to Basil T's
Brewpub and Italian Grill**

ranean and Italian dishes, but I like to throw in some Latin and Asian to spice things up," said Steve. "The daily specials allow us to do that without major alterations to the standard menu. Our regular customers demand that we keep their favorites available." As for his philosophy on food: "I believe in using fresh ingredients slow-cooked to bring out the deep flavors."

Unfortunately, beer dinners are not done on a regular basis. Steve's pairings of beers and food are exquisite, and we all enjoyed those they've held. I hope they will reconsider that policy.

Come in weekdays between 2 P.M. and 6 P.M. and enjoy the happy hour specials. You not only get $2 off the homemade beers and drinks and $1 off bottles, but also can chow down on a sumptuous buffet in the bar area . . . gratis. Nothing like free food to accompany discounted beer!

This was a regular destination for us for many years, until gas prices went through the roof and the 100-mile round-trip began to cost as much as the meal. Still, we make the excursion as often as we can to partake of the excellent cuisine and beer. We try to arrive for the early-bird specials and get a full meal for the cost of a lunch—an exceptional bargain.

The town is pretty much central to all areas of New Jersey, and it's an easy drive with plenty of parking and nearby shopping. Don't miss the full experience of Dave Hoffmann's beer, Steve Farley's cuisine, and the Mediterranean ambience. You'll find nothing better!

Opened: September 1997.

Owners: Pete and Peter Gregorakis.

Brewer: Dave Hoffmann.

System: 20-barrel Pub Brewing system, 1,000 barrels potential annual capacity.

Production: 300+ barrels in 2006.

Brewpub hours: Open every day, 11:30 A.M. to 1:30 A.M.

Tours: By appointment only.

Take-out beer: Half-gallon growlers.

Food: Traditional gourmet Italian. Some of the best Italian food you'll find anywhere. Fantastic early-bird menu with large portions and low prices.

Extras: Full bar with a great selection of wines. You can join the Mug Club also: A $25 yearly fee gets your 21-ounce mug filled for $2.95 at every visit. There is a VIP cigar lounge for members only. Membership costs $75 per year, which includes your club enrollment and 10 percent off cigar purchases. There is live music in the bar on weekends. Private rooms to hold meetings and parties are available.

Special considerations: Kids welcome. Vegetarian meals available. Handicapped-accessible.

Parking: On-premises lot.

Lodging in the area: Howard Johnson Hotel, 955 Hooper Avenue, Toms River, 732-244-1000; Holiday Inn, 290 Route 37 East, Toms River, 732-244-4000.

Area attractions: The **Ritacco Center** (1245 Old Freehold Road, Toms River, 732-818-8536) is a big, thirty-five-hundred-seat venue that presents top-flight entertainment acts. Adjoining Toms River is the city of **Seaside Heights,** a shore community with a beach and a boardwalk. There are amusement parks (Funtime Pier and Beach/ Casino Pier), stores, theaters, fishing, boating, and all the things you expect in a resort town. Go have some fun! If you want to play golf, check out the **Bey Lea Municipal Golf Course** (1536 North Bay

Avenue, Toms River, 732-349-0566) or **Cedar Creek at Berkeley Municipal Golf Course** (Tilton Boulevard, Bayville, 732-269-4460). **Other area beer sites:** Just up the road a quarter mile is a place that used to be a brewpub and still has the sign up to prove it. *Joshua Huddy's* (1250 Hooper Avenue, Toms River, 732-240-3640) appears to be one of those chain-style restaurants: bright, airy, and open. It has been in Toms River for the past twenty-eight years and is a popular spot for sports lovers to watch a game and shoppers from the Ocean County Mall across the street to stop and refresh themselves. It has a large bar, lots of sports paraphernalia everywhere, and nineteen TVs. Its eighteen taps, unfortunately, are filled with mostly mediocre selections. The menus look good, however, and you'll find a wide range of foods at reasonable prices. Another nearby location just off the Garden State Parkway and Route 37 is **The Office Restaurant and Lounge** (820 Main Street, Toms River, 732-349-0800). Not part of the chain that is permeating the northern part of the state, it is a little more upscale and has an eclectic menu, including a sushi and sashimi bar. The restaurant has a modern look, with a very large kidney-shaped bar. The beer selection here was the best I found in the area; not great, but one could make do with the few craft beers on tap.

If you want to take something back to your room, try **E-Z Liquors** (35 Route 37 East, Toms River, 732-341-3444) for a nice selection of esoteric wines and beers. You'll find more mainstream stuff at **Monaghan's Liquors** (1617 Route 37 East, Toms River, 732-270-6060); **Spirits Unlimited** (897 Fischer Boulevard, Toms River, 732-270-8338); and **Circle on the Square Liquors** (1930 Route 88, Brick, 732-458-5822).

Laird and Company

1 Laird Road, Scobeyville, NJ 07724
877-GET-LAIRD
www.lairdandcompany.com

You all know Yuengling: America's oldest brewery, dating back to 1829, and one of the oldest family-owned businesses in the country. I've made many trips to the Pottsville powerhouse. But recently, for the first time, I visited the country's oldest distillery, and it's a lot older than Yuengling. Tucked away in Scobeyville, a bucolic corner of Monmouth County, is Laird and Company, distillers of Laird's Applejack. They've been selling applejack since 1780.

"We know we were producing for family and friends before that," said Lisa Laird Dunn, vice president of sales and marketing and the ninth generation of the family that still owns 100 percent of this company. "But the first physical record is from 1780, Robert Laird's book of operations." Applejack was called "corpse reviver" and "Jersey Lightning," salutes to its potency and origins. It has been recognized as America's oldest native spirit; according to Lisa, "It predates bourbon."

Laird's doesn't distill in New Jersey anymore; the actual distilling takes place down in North Garden, Virginia, in the middle of the Shenandoah Valley apple country. Laird's bought that distillery after Repeal and moved all production there in the 1970s. "In the mid-seventies, there was a shortage of apples here," Lisa said. "We were surrounded by apple orchards, but now it's all housing. And the EPA regulations—even though we're a 100 percent natural product—made things very difficult."

It's not even easy in Virginia. "Nowadays, our apple choice is mainly what we can get," she said. "There's not a lot of apple orchards, and most of those are spoken for by large companies. We use the kinds of apples you'd find in the store: Red Delicious, Golden Delicious, Braeburn, Pippin, Stayman, and Winesap, and all native-grown. The most favored is the Winesap; it makes the best cider."

It's not cheap, either. It takes 7,000 pounds of apples to make 1 barrel of apple brandy. One bottle

Spirits produced: Laird's Applejack, Laird's Straight Apple Brandy Bottled in Bond 100 Proof, Laird's Old Apple Brandy, Laird's twelve-year-old Rare Apple Brandy.

of Laird's Applejack has 6 pounds of apples, but that's a blended product; it's 35 percent apple brandy and 65 percent grain neutral spirits. I'm drinking Laird's Bottled in Bond 100-proof Straight Apple Brandy as I write this: 20 pounds of apples in one bottle. I figure that's at least a month's worth of keeping the doctor away.

The apples are crushed and the cider is fermented naturally, with the yeast on the skins. Nothing at all is added. The cider goes to a pot still with a rectifying column and comes off the still at about 160 proof. Master distiller Lester "Mac" Clemens puts the distillate into used bourbon barrels, which are then aged in warehouses at the distillery and at the original site in New Jersey.

Aging is the important work. Distillation is finicky, technical work, and pressing apples for cider and then carefully shepherding it through fermentation is no picnic either. But the shape and size and construction of the warehouse, the climate and the siting, how you open or close the windows, and how you choose your barrels—that's how you make magic.

I've become quite familiar with the bourbon warehouses in Kentucky. The similarities between those warehouses and the warehouses at Laird's were striking. The same mold on the walls, the same construction, the same hardware—all that's not so surprising. But the smell, the atmosphere, heavy with the boozy bit that's always "osmosing" out through the barrel staves, called the "angel's share"—it was just like being in Bardstown, Kentucky.

Why did we include a distillery in a book about New Jersey's breweries? Honestly, one of the reasons was because it's a small book, and we wanted to give you your money's worth. But the main reason is because Laird's is unique. It is the oldest booze business in America, and it makes a product that has been associated with New Jersey for more than three hundred years.

If you're not familiar with Laird's Applejack, you should stop by your local New Jersey bar and make its acquaintance; we noted a bottle of Laird's at almost every bar we visited. It is bottled at 80 proof and is mostly used in applejack-specific cocktails like the Jack Rose. But it also substitutes nicely for bourbon in a Manhattan or Old-Fashioned, and that means that the recent surge in interest in "brown goods"—bourbon, rye, Canadian whisky—has been good for applejack. "I'm loving it," Lisa

The Pick: I like the twelve-year-old, and the bottle's beautiful. But after trying all of them (Lisa gave me a bottle of twelve-year-old, and then I stopped on the way home and bought one of each of the others, I was so taken with the whole place), I've got to say I like the full apple authority of the bottled in bond Straight Apple Brandy. It's young enough that you're getting some of the rawness, but old enough to tame it, and it's a great drink on the rocks with some soda.

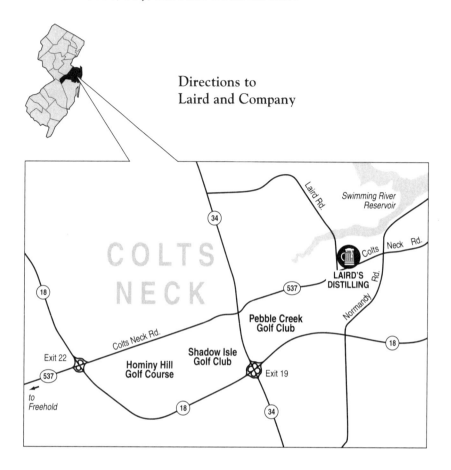

Directions to
Laird and Company

said, sporting a wide grin. "It's all helping: interest in whiskey, our 225th anniversary in 2005, and our new package."

Applejack is the basic product, the flagship, but Laird's sells three other apple liquors you might be interested in. Besides the Bottled in Bond brandy I mentioned earlier, they also have a seven-and-a-half-year-old apple brandy at 80 proof and an absolutely delicious twelve-year-old Rare Apple Brandy. The brandies make a great drink straight up in a snifter or mixed with a splash of water or seltzer.

Following other, much larger companies in the survival strategy of the new playing field of drinks, Laird and Company has diversified, now producing, bottling, and importing a wide variety of products: wines, spirits, cordials, even olive oils and vinegars.

"Only 5 percent of the business is applejack anymore," Lisa said, "but it's the heart and soul of the business. It's our heritage." Part of that heritage is also the Scobeyville site, with its low brick warehouses, original offices, and whitewashed family house. The family plans to turn the house into a visitors center—and they must, this place is grand—but as Lisa said, a small family business can always find something to spend money on instead of repairing old buildings.

As I drove away, past the Colt's Neck Inn, where that first recorded sale of Laird's applejack was made, I felt like I was leaving a little corner of Kentucky. Laird's has that same slow, genial feeling, an air of being outside of time, unaffected by the rush of modern life. Believe me, you can get that same feeling with a few glasses of Laird's Apple Brandy.

Jersey lightning. Bring on the storm.

Opened: Sometime prior to 1780.
Owner: The Laird family.
Distiller: Lester "Mac" Clemens.
Production: The family does not release sales figures.
Tours: Not available yet, but plans are pending.
Extras: Try some classic Applejack cocktails. Jack Rose: 2 ounces Applejack, 1 ounce lemon juice, 1/2 ounce grenadine. Shake with ice and strain into a cocktail glass. Jersey Devil: 1 ounce Applejack, 1/3 ounce Cointreau, 1/3 ounce lime juice, 1/3 ounce cranberry juice, 1/3 teaspoon superfine sugar. Shake with ice and strain. Stone Fence: Pour 1 ounce Applejack into a tall glass filled with ice. Top off with apple cider and stir.
Area attractions: There's not really much here. You'll find an orchard and market across the street, a good deli at the **Colt's Neck Inn,** and some farm stands in season. With no tours currently going on, that's probably about all you need. Have a good drive in the pretty country, and try to relax.

Tun Tavern

In the Sheraton Hotel, 2 Miss America Way,
Atlantic City, NJ 08401
609-347-7800
www.tuntavern.com

One of the most common questions about Atlantic City is, "Is there life outside the casinos?" For good beer drinkers, the choices inside *and* outside the casinos are few. The one oasis in this desert is the Tun Tavern. Opened in January 1998 as part of the Convention Center–Sheraton Hotel project, Atlantic City's only brewpub began brewing operations for a small but eager group of beer aficionados.

The venue had three things going for it: location, location, location. Across the street from the Atlantic City Convention Center and attached to the Sheraton Hotel, it has a built-in clientele when a convention is in town, but it has to draw in the locals to firm up its off-season business. Being at the entrance and exit of the Atlantic City Expressway and across the street from the train station certainly helps with accessibility for visitors and locals alike. The train to and from Philadelphia runs a regular schedule, with several strategic stops along the way.

Historically speaking, the original Tun Tavern was the first brewhouse built in Philadelphia, in 1685. It was also acknowledged as the first Masonic meeting place and later the birthplace of the U.S. Marine Corps. Company president Monty Dahm, a Mason and former Marine, uses this venue as a marketing tool to members of those organizations. He supports websites geared toward the corps and keeping in touch with fellow Marines. Every year on November 10, they hold a special event celebrating the birthday of the U.S. Marine Corps, with food and drink specials, a piper, color guard, and birthday cake. All year long, they solicit support for the Marine Corps Scholarship Foundation, which aids children of Marines and former Marines.

Before opening the brewpub, Monty formed a separate nonprofit corporation, leased the Tun Tav-

Beers brewed: Year-round: Tun Lite, Irish Red, Devil Dog Pale, Bullies Brown, Leather-Neck Stout, All-American IPA. Seasonals: Oktoberfest, Hefeweizen, Doppelbock, Pumpkin Ale, Biere de Tun, Ryebock Lager, Freedom Ale Barleywine, Quad, Vienna Lager, etc.

ern trademark from the Marines, and produced Tun Tavern Lager at Lion Brewing in Wilkes-Barre, Pennsylvania. It was sold mainly in the Philadelphia area but came to a quick demise. The Tun Tavern Brewing Company supports a foundation to rebuild the Tun Tavern in Philadelphia as a museum and hopes that someday it will come to fruition. This foundation received a fifty-year lease on property at 2nd and Spruce, where the planned construction will occur.

The Pick: You'll have to excuse me—I had to pick more than one. All-American IPA, at 50 IBU and 6.2 percent ABV, made with all American ingredients, has a crisp, citrusy hop bitterness that's a hophead's delight. The Biere de Tun is my favorite seasonal, vinous with a wonderful malty sweet finish. Finally, the Freedom Ale, a barleywine, is aged for six months in bourbon barrels and served starting on 9/11 each year.

Then came the offer to build a brewpub in the new Atlantic City Sheraton. Monty couldn't resist the temptation. His business acumen told him this was the place. Monty remembered, "I came this close to taking over the Red Bell [brewpub] site at the Reading Terminal Market [in Philadelphia] as a second location, but it just didn't feel right. If I find a place that does, I'll consider it." He made a good call; that site has been problematic for years, and it recently closed and reopened without the brewery.

The brewmaster, Tim Kelly, took over the kettles in May 2007 and has built up a list of well-brewed flagship beers and some tasty seasonals. He spends most of his time brewing Tun Lite, the biggest seller, but Tim is especially fond of lagers and plans on brewing as many of those styles as tank space will permit.

"I've always wanted to be able to brew what I like instead of what my boss wanted," Tim said. "Now that I have the chance, lagers of every style will be pouring from the tanks. Planning for them makes all the difference." I've had his Oktoberfest and Vienna Lager, so I can say firsthand that they are worth the time he spends on them.

His desire to make his own mark at the Tun has led him to tweak the flagship recipes a bit. "I figure, why make the same thing all the time? I will experiment with different hops and malts in the Pale and the IPA to make them a little distinctive once in a while. I don't think the customers will mind. As a matter of fact, I'm hoping it will get more geeks in to try the reformulations."

Though regular tours are not held, if you stop in and Tim isn't busy, I'm sure he'll explain the process to you. Be sure to take home a growler or three of Tim's creations to enjoy at your leisure.

Besides their own products, the Tun serves several selections from the megabrewers as well as providing a full bar. The wine selection is minimal but superb and should please even the most discriminating

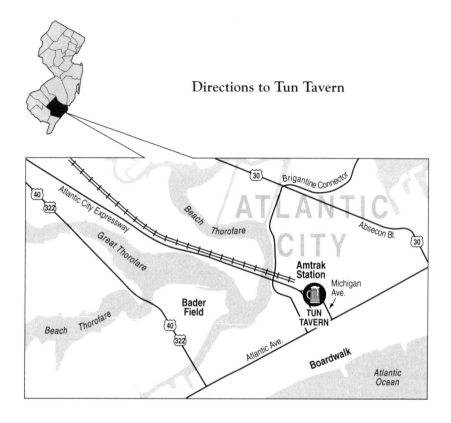

Directions to Tun Tavern

wine lover. A nice collection of single malts rounds out the choices at the bar.

The restaurant itself is quite an impressive sight. The entryway where you are greeted by the hostess is adorned with Tun Tavern merchandise, but your eyes are immediately drawn to the glass enclosure above the bar that holds the fermenters. All that glittering stainless steel! It's an exceptional vista to all, except the brewer, who has to navigate the narrow stairs from the brewhouse on a regular basis. At the rear of the facility stands the heart and soul of the pub and the reason many make the visit: the brewery. Large windows front the room so that you can watch the brewer ply his trade while you enjoy the fruits of his labor at the bar.

The open atrium dining area is quite spacious and houses a very large horseshoe bar that can accommodate a multitude of thirsty patrons. Five flat-screen TVs surround the bar to keep you up-to-date with the latest news, sports, or financial matters. For those seeking a little more privacy, there are large enclosed booths. When weather permits, you can enjoy the outdoor deck, with breathtaking views of Atlantic City's casino skyline. Plans are under way to enclose this deck for year-round use.

The menu is an eclectic mix of old standards and some unique combos. If you're looking for pub grub or a full meal, the Tun can fill the bill. From appetizers to sandwiches to Angus steaks or seafood entrées, the freshly prepared food will impress you with its quantity and quality. In addition to the regular menu, there are special theme nights during the week that offer an extended menu with appropriate selections. And if you haven't had enough, the exciting dessert menu will finish you off with selections such as Strawberry Mile High Fantasy or Chocolate Decadence. Definitely not for the carb watcher! Several times a year, beer dinners show off both the chef's prowess and the brewer's skill, melding the two into magnificent culinary events.

The VIP Program gives the regulars discounted beer every day and dining specials during the week. Beer dinners, seasonal brews, entertainment, and special offers have brought many into the fold, and the brewpub has become a popular lunch and after-work watering hole, as well as a destination for the curious beer drinker who has never heard of good beer in Atlantic City.

Just down the street is The Walk, a newly opened shopping area comprising eight blocks of the nation's best outlets in a safe, well-lit area. Expansion of this complex is an ongoing project, with new stores opening regularly. You can build up an appetite shopping and then stop in for some refreshment or a complete meal. Four hours of free parking are available across the street with validation.

So when you visit Casino City, be sure to stop in and see what's brewing in our part of the state. You always come out a winner!

Opened: January 1998.
Owner: Monty Dahm, president and CEO, Tun Tavern Brewing Company.
Brewer: Tim Kelly.
System: 10-barrel Newlands system, annual capacity 1,000 barrels.
Production: 550 barrels in 2006.
Brewpub hours: Seven days a week, 11:30 A.M. to 2 A.M.; this *is* Atlantic City.
Tours: As requested, if brewer is available.
Take-out beer: Half-gallon growlers.

Food: Eclectic mix of traditional and modern. A full menu with an array of appetizers, salads, oversize sandwiches, Black Angus steaks, and seafood entrées. The huge desserts are sinful.

Extras: Live music on Friday and Saturday, plus live reggae on Wednesday. Karaoke on Thursdays.

Special considerations: Kids welcome. Limited choices for vegetarians: salads, veggie appetizers, and some pasta. Handicapped-accessible.

Parking: Free with validation at lot across the street.

Lodging in the area: You can stay right at the brewpub in the Sheraton Hotel, 609-344-3535. There's also Caesar's Casino, 2100 Pacific Avenue, Atlantic City, 800-443-0104; Trump Plaza Casino, Mississippi and the Boardwalk, Atlantic City, 800-677-7378; Econo Lodge Boardwalk, 117 South Kentucky Avenue, Atlantic City, 609-344-9093.

Area attractions: There's something for everyone in Atlantic City. Gambling is the main attraction at the eight casinos on the Boardwalk and three more on the bay side, but many have daily variety shows and regular concerts from the best entertainers in the business. The Tun is now conveniently located one block from a new outlet center, *The Walk,* eight blocks of outlet stores and entertainment venues (www.acoutlets.com). The *Boardwalk* is a treat for those who are looking to walk or shop, with attractions such as Ripley's Believe It or Not Museum, Hard Rock Café, House of Blues, Atlantic City Art Center, and the Quarter at Tropicana. There's also the beach for summer enjoyment and quiet winter walks in the sand. In the summer, the local baseball team, the AC Surf, plays semipro ball in a beautiful stadium and has fireworks displays often. Restaurants and buffets for every taste abound both in and out of the casinos. Dance clubs and taverns contribute to the wild nightlife in this resort town. Boat rides and fishing in season, an early-morning bicycle ride on the Boardwalk, a walk up the Absecon Lighthouse in Atlantic City, golfing at championship courses, and even miniature golf are some of the diversions available to the visitor. Get information on them all from the Atlantic City Convention and Visitors Authority (www.atlantic citynj.com, 888-AC-VISIT).

The *Historic Towne of Smithville,* a group of restaurants and shops in a restored Colonial town, is only ten minutes outside of Atlantic City. It's a wonderful family outing.

Ocean City is fifteen minutes away, with a Boardwalk of its own replete with rides and other amusements. But don't look for beer there—Ocean City is dry, always has been. The resort town of **Wildwood** is half an hour south, with water parks, amusements, and another Boardwalk. Historic **Cape May** lies a speedy forty-five minutes down the Garden State Parkway, with access to the ferry to Lewes, Delaware, and tax-free shopping in the **Rehoboth Beach Outlets.**

For the golfer, the **Seaview Marriott** (Route 9, Absecon, 800-932-8000) has two beautiful courses; there are two courses at **Blue Heron Pines and Pines East** (550 West Country Club Drive, Cologne, 888-478-2746); and the **Mays Landing Country Club** (1855 Cates Road, Mays Landing, 609-641-4411) has the best golf for the buck. There are many more top courses in the area. Visit www.gacga.com for more info.

Other area beer sites: With fifty taps and 101 bottles, you can't go wrong at **Firewaters** (Tropicana Casino and Resort, just off the Boardwalk). The beer menu is dynamic and changes with the seasons. Deli food is available at the attached Adam Good Deli. **Ri~Ra** (The Quarter in the Tropicana Casino and Resort, 609-348-8600) is as close to an authentic Irish pub as you'll see anywhere. As a matter of fact, it *is* an actual pub shipped over from Ireland piece by piece. Here you'll find authentic Irish cuisine and beer—Guinness, Smithwick's, Harp—plus some good Irish whiskeys. If one Irish pub isn't good enough for you, the **Irish Pub** (164 Saint James Place, Atlantic City, 609-344-9063) is another with all the fixings. **W. L. Goodfellows** (310 East White Horse Pike, U.S. Route 30, Absecon, 609-652-1942) has the largest and most complete menu I have ever seen. Their beer list is also notable, with a selection of local and national crafts and imports on tap and in the bottle, plus an additional nice assortment of bottled Belgian beer. **Trinity Pub** (The Pier at Caesar's, Atlantic City Boardwalk at Michigan Avenue) is yet another authentic Irish pub with the usual suspects.

Brewer's Apprentice

179 South Street, Freehold, NJ 07728
732-863-9411
www.brewapp.com

Since 1996

Where You're The Brewer!

Tired of making the drive to your local package store and staring down the beer aisle overwhelmed by all the choices? Always wanted to try your hand at homebrewing but didn't know where to start or get equipment? Or are you not brewing in the summer because you have no place cool enough to ferment it?

Then Brewer's Apprentice in Freehold is for you. It is the state's only brew-on-premises. Here is your one-stop shop for producing the beer, wine, cider, or mead of your choice with professional help or purchasing your homebrewing equipment and supplies. Homebrew shops are a rare sight in these parts, and here is one of the best. Stop in during working hours or order online, whichever is most convenient.

If you've never homebrewed before, the experience will make you see what you've been missing all these years. When you're done, invite your friends over and open up a couple of bottles and tell them you made it. Look at the surprised expressions on their faces. Better yet, make your brewday a party. Bring all your friends with you, and make different recipes and share them. Variety *is* the spice of life.

The best part about brewing at this location is that all the ingredients are right here and there is no cleanup. That's right . . . whatever mess you make is joyfully cleaned up by the crew! That alone makes it worth a visit.

I think the hardest thing is deciding what you want to brew. Making that decision prior to scheduling your appointment is highly recommended. That way, when you arrive, all you have to decide is which recipe you'll use. The list of recipes at the Brewer's Apprentice is quite extensive, more than 180 in all, almost any style and variation you can think of. They have collected a multitude of these from some of the best brewers in the area for you to re-create. Bring your own if you like, but let them know ahead of time what ingredients you'll need to be sure they have them on hand on the day of your appointment. Jo-Ellen,

Barbara, and Penny are more than happy to accommodate whatever it is you would like to try.

The ingredients and the use of all the brewing equipment and twenty-four labels are all included in the price. Extra labels are available at a small charge. You can choose the premade designs for your labels or come up with something different and innovative. Using the bottles for a special event or as gifts? Customize the labels to suit your needs. If you need some help with the design, for a small fee, the ladies will use your picture or graphics to produce a custom label for you.

Your batch will result in your taking home seventy-two 22-ounce bottles of beer. The bottles used to be part of the package price, but because of volatility in the glass market, they are now extra and currently cost $4 per twelve-bottle case. You can return with your bottles on your next visit and save the cost of new ones—just be sure they're properly cleaned and sanitized.

So you've arrived for your appointment and chosen a recipe? Then you're ready to get started! First, state law requires that you fill out a brewing license and pay a fee of $20 once a year for the right to make an alcoholic beverage in New Jersey. This permits you to make no more than 200 gallons during that period. The brewery will help you file this form, but a check is required to be sent to the Alcohol Beverage Control.

Once you've completed the paperwork and made all your decisions, the next step is to gather and weigh out all the ingredients you'll be needing for your brewday. The kettle is filled with 15 gallons of water and brought up to the proper temperature. Now the real brewing begins. Specialty grains are the first item to go into the vessel and are steeped for a while. When that step is complete, you remove the grains and add the extracts and hops to begin the boil. Now's the time to relax. But watch the kettle! It might boil over, and they'll have a mess to clean up. Also, if you have another hops addition, watch that clock.

After the boil is done, the wort is cooled through a heat exchanger and racked into a fermentation tank and the yeast added. Your brewday is over, and now the anticipation starts.

Your beer will ferment for two weeks, wine longer, and it's closely watched by the crew awaiting your return to finish. The day you return for bottling, the beer will be filtered and all ready to package. Bottling is not the favorite task for most people, but the brewery's equipment makes it quick and easy. The counterpressure filler purges the oxygen from the bottle with carbon dioxide and then fills it, leaving no air behind to spoil your creation. Cap the bottle and your beer is ready for transport. If you prefer to bring your own ball-lock Corny kegs, the old-

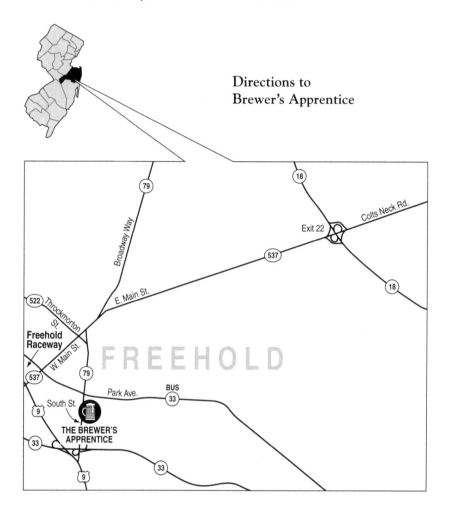

Directions to
Brewer's Apprentice

style soda canisters, the beer can be transferred into them and you can save the time and effort of bottling.

I can guarantee that you will enjoy the experience and will want to return to try other recipes. You'll be surprised at how many friends you have when you tell them you're making beer!

Opened: December 1996.
Owners: Barbara Hamara, Penny van Doorn, Jo-Ellen Ford.
Brewer: You! (Don't worry, brewer Ron Mahler is on hand to help out.)
System: Five 15-gallon systems from the Brew Store.
Hours: Monday and Wednesday through Friday, 1 P.M. to 8 P.M.; Saturday and Sunday, 10 A.M. to 4 P.M.; closed Tuesday.

Tours: Available on weekends by appointment after 4 P.M.

Special considerations: Handicapped-accessible. Not suggested for children, for safety reasons.

Parking: On-site spaces.

Lodging in the area: Freehold Gardens Hotel, 50 Gibson Place, Freehold, 732-780-3870; Hepburn House B&B, 15 Monument Street, Freehold, 732-462-7696.

Area attractions: Freehold was the site of the Battle of Monmouth in 1778, the fight where New Jersey heroine Molly Pitcher made her fame, taking over a man's job in an artillery crew to continue fighting the British. You can learn more at the **Monmouth Battlefield State Park,** 3 miles west of Freehold on State Business Route 3, where there's a visitors center and the restored 1710 Craig House (visitors center is open daily, 9 A.M. to 4 P.M., 732-462-9616). If you'd prefer something a bit more lively, you'll find harness racing most of the year at **Freehold Raceway** (U.S. Route 9 and State Route 3, 732-462-3800, www.freeholdraceway.com), which claims to be the nation's oldest half-mile harness track, dating from 1853 and still kicking.

Other area beer sites: Not much. Better bring it along if you plan to indulge.

A word about . . .

Brewing Beer

You don't need to know much about beer to enjoy it. After all, you probably don't understand how the electronic fuel injection on your car really works . . . but you know that when you stomp on the gas, the car's gonna go!

But if you're going to go to the breweries in this book, you'll have to know how to talk shop with the bartenders and tour guides and not embarrass yourself on the tour. More important, knowing about the brewing process can help you understand how and why beer tastes the way it does. It's like seeing the ingredients used in cooking a dish and realizing where the flavors came from. Once you understand the recipe for beer, other things become more clear.

First off, beer is any fermented beverage made from malted grain. Beer as we know it, in the European tradition that is the dominant model, is made from four basic ingredients: water, hops, yeast, and a malted grain, generally barley. Other ingredients may be added, such as sugars, spices, fruits, and vegetables, but they are extras. The oft-quoted Bavarian Reinheitsgebot (purity law), dating from 1516, limited brewers to using only water, hops, and barley malt; yeast had not yet been discovered.

In the beginning, the malt is cracked in a mill to make a grist. The grist is mixed with water and heated (or "mashed") to convert the starches in the grain to sugars (see *decoction* and *infusion* in the glossary). Then the hot, sugary water—now called wort—is strained out of the mash. It is boiled in the brewkettle, where hops are added to balance the sweetness with their characteristic bitterness and sprightly aroma. The wort is strained, cooled, and pumped to a fermenter, where yeast is added.

A lager beer ferments slow and cool, whereas an ale ferments warmer and faster. After fermentation, the beer will either be force-carbonated or naturally carbonated and aged. When it is properly mature for its style, the beer is bottled, canned, kegged, or, in a brewpub, sent to a large serving tank. And then we drink it. Happy ending!

Naturally, it isn't quite that simple. The process varies somewhat from brewery to brewery. That's what makes beers unique. There are also major differences in the ways microbrewers and mainstream brewers brew beer. One well-known distinction has to do with the use of nonbarley grains, specifically corn and rice, in the brewing process. Some microbrewers have made a big deal of their Reinheitsgebot, proudly displaying slogans like "Barley, hops, water, and yeast—and that's all!" Mainstream brewers like Anheuser-Busch and Miller add significant portions of corn, rice, or both. Beer geeks howl about how these adjuncts make the beer inferior. Of course, the same geeks often rave about Belgian ales, which have a regular farrago of ingredients forbidden by the Reinheitsgebot.

Mainstream brewers boast about the quality of the corn grits and brewer's rice they use, while microbrewers chide them for using "cheap" adjunct grains and "inferior" six-row barley. Truth is, they're both right . . . and they're both wrong.

Barley, like beer, comes in two main types: two-row and six-row. The names refer to the rows of kernels on the heads of the grain. Six-row grain gives a greater yield per acre but has more husks on smaller kernels, which can give beer an unpleasant astringency. Two-row has plumper kernels with less husk but costs significantly more. Each has its place and adherents.

When brewing began in America, farmers and brewers discovered that six-row barley did much better than two-row in our climate and soil types. Two-row barley grown the same way as it had been in Europe produced a distinctly different malt. This became especially troublesome when the craze for pale lagers swept America in the mid-nineteenth century. The hearty ales they replaced had broad flavors from hops and yeast that easily compensated for these differences. But pale lagers are showcases for malt character, and small differences in the malt mean big differences in beer taste.

Brewers adapted and used what they had. They soon found that a small addition of corn or brewer's rice to the mash lightened the beer, smoothed out the husky astringency of the six-row malt, and gave the beer a crispness similar to that of the European pale lagers. Even though using these grains required the purchase, operation, and maintenance of additional equipment (cookers, storage silos, and conveyors), almost every American brewer did it. Some say they overdid it, as the percentages of adjuncts in the beer rose over the years. Is a beer that is 30 percent corn still a pilsner?

Microbrewers say adjunct grains are cheap substitutes for barley malt. In terms of yield, corn and brewer's rice are less expensive than two-row barley, but they are still high-quality grains. Similarly, six-row barley is not inherently inferior to two-row; it is just not as well suited to the brewing of some styles of beer. Mainstream brewers have adapted their brewing processes to six-row barley. The difference is in the beer those processes produce.

What else should you know? As we said earlier, almost all the beers in the world fall into one of two types: ales and lagers. There are many subdivisions in those two types—stout, bock, IPA, pilsner, and so on—but they're all one or the other basic type. The big sellers in the world, the familiar names, are almost all lagers, with Guinness and Newcastle all alone as ales. On the other hand, the most familiar American micro-brews are all ales, except the biggest one, Samuel Adams Boston . . . Lager.

What's the difference? Simple, on the surface: Ales ferment and age at warmer temperatures than lagers, and lagers usually take longer to age because of that. There are some more technical differences, but that's the real one.

So what? Can you taste that? You bet. Think of it in terms of jungles and forests. Warm-fermenting ales are like jungles: a lot of diverse, intense flavors and aromas, pushed into busy life by all that heat. Life explodes in weird, wonderful abundance, much like the flavors you get laid on top of the basic ingredients in an ale fermentation: nuts, fruits, spices, butter, earthiness, all from the hot, excited yeast. Ale brewers are champions of this complexity.

Lagers are like vast northern pine and oak forests. It's cold there, things grow slower, and the habitat is simpler: miles of spruce, herds of deer. Rabbits. A hawk. Life follows slower, straighter paths, though no less powerful. Step outside your cabin and take a deep breath: wood smoke, warm earth, and a heady rush of pine. That's lager: a beer that gets out of the way and lets you taste the malt and hops it's made of. A lager brewer will tell you that there's nowhere to hide when you make lager beer; the unadorned nature of the beer makes flaws stand out immediately.

There are other differences, but at the heart of it, it's simple. Warm and complex, cool and smooth—kind of like women and men. It's good to have both, for different occasions.

Among small brewers in America, ale brewers outnumber lager brewers by more than ten to one. Given that lagers are by far the most popular beers in the world, how did this come to be? Tom Pastorius of Penn Brewing in Pittsburgh puts it quite simply: "More ale is being made because it's cheaper, easier, and more flexible." Hard words, per-haps, but the facts bear them out.

After lagers are fermented, they undergo an extended aging period of at least three weeks at low temperatures. The cooling and the tank time required add energy costs and decrease turnover. In the same amount of time, it would be possible to put twice as much ale through those tanks. Add the energy and labor costs of the more complicated decoction brewing process used for lagers, and you wind up with a product that costs substantially more to brew than ales but has to be priced the same. No wonder there are more ale brewers!

American beer enthusiasts are slowly coming around to microbrewed lagers. The pioneering Pennsylvania brewer Carol Stoudt attributes their hesitation to a megabrew backlash: "People who have had nothing but bland lagers for years want the extremes: heavy-handed hops, fruit beers, even smoked beers. As their palates become more sophisticated, they'll come around to appreciate the subtleties of a good lager beer."

If you'd like to see the difference temperature can make, you can do a little lager taste-testing at Triumph, where Jay Misson has made sure their award-winning lagers get on the brewing rotation, or your favorite Cricket Hill outlet, whose American Lager has a strong local following.

SOMETHING ABOUT
A RIVERSIDE TOWN
The Western Waters

Don't hold it against me, but when we first moved to Bucks County, Pennsylvania, and my wife was commuting to Princeton, I was given to saying, way too often, "You know, this part of New Jersey's just as nice as Pennsylvania!" Must have endeared me to the local citizenry.

I meant it in the nicest of ways. I was a Pennsylvania chauvinist in those days, but travel, my wife's family, and finally, researching this book have broken me down. There are parts of New Jersey I'm really happy to visit, maybe even could call home, and not just because they're like Pennsylvania.

But this closest part of New Jersey to me, the land along the Delaware River, has a special quality that's more than its proximity. There is something about a riverside town—whether in the urban knot of Camden and its sprawling ring of suburbs (more properly Philadelphia's suburbs), among the neighborhoods of Trenton, or one of the little gems like Lambertville or Milford—that makes it special. A good-size river provides not only a vista, but also countless recreation possibilities as well as the simple pleasures of walking the banks and dabbling your feet in the flow.

River-town folks live differently; they have a division in their neighborhood that can be crossed only by a bridge, and it molds their lives. Cares are different when a flood could change everything; cooperation becomes more important, and enjoying the good days.

The Delaware was an important river in American history, crucial during the Revolution. Washington famously crossed it in a last-chance gamble in the waning days of 1776 as his battered army was melting away, betting everything on the opposing Hessian mercenaries in Trenton being off their guard on a snowy post-Christmas morning. Not only did he win big, he played it like a native and parlayed his win into a shot up the road into Princeton, where the rebels won again. The British let him slip away, the fortunes of the rebellion and its army restored by the stunning success of Washington's Crossing.

The river later supported canals and fishing—including a long run as a major source of caviar—and eventually came to be a great recreational resource. From Delaware Bay all the way up to the Delaware Water Gap National Recreation Area, sailboats, speedboats, Jet-Skis, and canoes cut the waters of the river; fishers strive to snag passing shad; and thousands walk and pedal along the banks, enjoying the scenery and the peace.

We'll start down in Camden, in the big shadow of Philadelphia. Camden has had problems for years with violence and blight, but the waterfront is getting things together with the revamped **Adventure Aquarium** and **Battleship *New Jersey*** attractions. Camden is the home of Campell's Soup; condensed soup was invented here in the 1800s, and the company has remained. They sponsored **Campbell Field,** the old-style stadium of the Camden Riversharks minor-league baseball team (856-963-2600, www.riversharks.com). Want big-name entertainment? The **Tweeter Center** (1 Harbour Boulevard, 856-365-1300) is both a twenty-five-thousand-seat amphitheater for open-air concerts against the Philly skyline and a much smaller theater for local acts, a great venue in either case.

The big belt of suburbs around Camden has much to offer, and you'll find more details in the Flying Fish entry. In keeping with our theme, though, you should know about the **Indian King Tavern Museum** (223 East Kings Highway, Haddonfield, 856-429-6792, www.levins.com/tavern .html). This is an original building, not a reconstruction, and it's a real tavern dating from 1750. Taverns in that period were centers of public life, and the Indian King was an important one: The New Jersey Assembly met here in 1777, after the armies of Washington and Cornwallis had damaged their meeting hall in Trenton, to declare New Jersey an independent state. It has been a New Jersey historic site—the first—since 1903, but sadly, you can't get a drink there, only memories and education, and maybe a little pride in tavernkeepers!

"Trenton Makes, the World Takes," says the sign on the green truss bridge known to locals as the "Trenton Makes Bridge," and it used to be so true. Trenton was not just the state capital, it also was home to a huge porcelain industry in "sanitary fixtures," steel, firearms, wire rope at John Roebling's mill (the cables on the Brooklyn Bridge were made in Trenton), and foods like Taylor Pork Roll and Trenton Oyster Crackers (River Horse Brewing is located in an old TOC bakery in Lambertville).

Things changed, and now Trenton is largely the state capital. The Mill Hill historic district has some nice architecture to look at, and there's the **Mercer County Waterfront Park** (on Route 29, just south of Route 1, 609-394-3300, www.trentonthunder.com), home of the Trenton Thunder, a New York Yankees AA farm team. You'll also find the state and city museums, the **Trenton Battle Monument** (North Broad and North Warren Streets, open Saturday and Sunday only, 609-737-0623), and tours of the **New Jersey State House** (www.njleg .state.nj.us).

But for me, the real reason to go to Trenton is to eat. **Chambersburg,** known to locals as the Burg, has the best concentration of Italian restaurants in a state jam-packed with Italian restaurants. You'll have a hard time not finding a good one. Some of the classics: **Amici Milano** (Chestnut and Roebling Avenues, 609-396-6300); **Marsillo's** (541 Roebling Avenue, 609-695-1916); **Diamonds** (132 Kent Street, 609-393-1000); and the much more informal **Rossi's Bar and Grille** (501 Morris Avenue, 609-394-9089), which is the only place where you're liable to get more than beer and light beer to choose from (and you might want to skip the Italian and order the awesome Rossiburger).

Don't want to get that involved in your food? Pick up some take-out at **DeLorenzo's** (530 Hudson Street, 609-695-9534), the place to go for that Trenton specialty, tomato pie. Tomato pie? Think pizza, only without all the mozzarella; tomato pie is about the bright red sauce and tomatoes and the crisp, slightly smoky crust. There's cheese, but it's lighter, and on the bottom, with a sprinkling of Parmesan on top. Nothing else like it. Oh, and be forewarned: DeLorenzo's doesn't have bathrooms. Plan accordingly.

Princeton is not far from Trenton or the river, with its great university and thriving scene of small restaurants, shops, and cultural centers like the **McCarter Theater,** which brings theater, dance, and music presentations to a wonderful small space (91 University Place, 888-278-7932, www.mccarter.org). The **Princeton Battlefield State Park** preserves the site where Washington's troops clashed with the British troops of Lord Cornwallis and General Mercer died of a British bayonet wound—several, actually (500 Mercer Road). You'll want to walk the beautiful **Princeton University** campus and take time to visit the university's **Art Museum** (McCormick Hall, 609-258-3788, www.princeton artmuseum.org), with free admission and a collection that ranges from Roman mosaics to Andy Warhol's *Blue Marilyn.*

On up the river now, and you'll find small towns linked by the two-lane River Road, which parallels the river and the **Delaware and Raritan Canal State Park,** a restored old canal with a towpath perfect for walking and biking. You may find me there on my bike; it's a beautiful ride beside the river. You'll pass through Titusville, Lambertville, Stockton, Frenchtown, and Milford, villages of varying sizes and offerings, and all worth stopping the car and walking around. There are shops—antiques, mostly—bars and restaurants, and B&Bs tucked into the corners, and always the river.

There's just something about a riverside town. Big or small, there's history, and quiet, beauty, and always possibilities for the day. Maybe, if you know where to look, you might find a good beer or two as well.

River Horse Brewing Company

80 Lambert Lane, Lambertville, NJ 08530
609-397-7776
www.riverhorse.com

Classic Ales & Lagers

"What's Past Is Prologue." I did my history master's thesis on a subject that required me to use papers kept at the National Archives in Washington. Every day I went there over the two months of my research, I saw those big words carved over the main entrance. It's a quote from *The Tempest*, and it was always a reassurance of my purpose: setting the future in perspective by explaining where the present came from.

I kept that in mind when I sat down to talk with the two guys who'd just bought River Horse, Glenn Bernabeo and Chris Walsh. River Horse had been open for eleven years when they bought it, and the way it had been run and what it had done was the prologue to this new chapter. I wanted to get an idea of what we could expect.

The prologue? River Horse was started in 1996 by the Bryan brothers, Jim, Jack, and Tim. They set up shop down Lambert Lane in the old OTC oys-

Beers brewed: Year-round: River Horse Lager, Hop Hazard, Special ESB Ale, Tripel Horse, Pennbrook Lager. Seasonals: Belgian Freeze, Summer Blonde, plus new beers for spring and fall.

ter cracker factory, a big brick building that Jack said already had "drains in all the right places." I was there with my buddy Mike Gates at the opening, a gala affair in the brewery. The Bryans were naturally excited, although it seemed as though a lot of the people present weren't quite sure what was really going on and thought there should be more to drink than just beer.

That's typical. Lambertville and New Hope, the Pennsylvania town a five-minute walk away across the New Hope–Lambertville Toll Supported Bridge (which is, oddly enough, free), have always been a bit behind the curve beerwise and still are, even now that both of them have breweries. (Triumph has a brewpub in New Hope.) The Inn of the Hawke was a lone outpost of beer variety in this area for a long time.

The Pick: The most common complaint you hear from the geekerie about River Horse is that the beers are everyday, commonplace, and boring. The two Belgian types, the Tripel Horse and Belgian Freeze, give the lie to those judgments. Tripel Horse is lively, zesty, and yet creamy smooth, a more classic tripel than most folks probably realize. Belgian Freeze stands on the other side: mellow, rich, and with an intriguing complexity of sweet and spicy flavors from the special malts and Belgian yeast strain.

The Bryans persevered, and River Horse continued to brew solid, clean beers. As you might expect, when a beer guy uses the words "solid, clean beers," what he means is that they're well made but not particularly exciting. "Competent" is another word, and maybe another would be "cautious." I never had a bad River Horse beer, but there weren't many that excited me either. Two that did were the Tripel Horse (see the Pick) and the now-retired Roebling Bock, and I hoped for more success, but nothing much happened.

Then came news that the brewery was for sale, followed soon by the names of Bernabeo and Walsh as the buyers. I got in touch with Glenn Bernabeo, and we set up a meeting.

The first question I asked was why two merger and acquisition guys (Walsh and Bernabeo were partners at SSG Capital Advisors) had bought a brewery. "We were serving smaller companies," said Glenn. "When we sold SSG in 2006, we were looking for another challenge. We wanted to make something, something that meant something to both of us"

"That's right," Chris agreed. "We'd been watching other people do it, helping other people do it. We wanted to do it ourselves."

"We were looking for a business that was three things," Glenn explained. "It had to be in manufacturing, making something we cared about, and not be a situation where we had to cut fat, cut losses and jobs. That was just not something we wanted to have to do. We both have liked craft beer for a long time, so when this came along . . ."

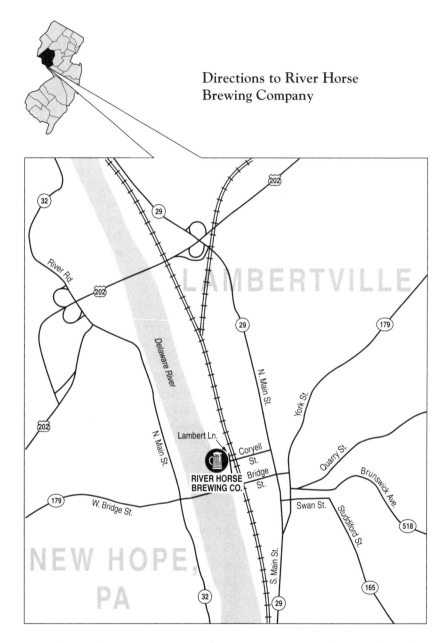

Directions to River Horse Brewing Company

What did River Horse need? "You name it," Glenn said. "They needed fuel, capital fuel." The brewery couldn't produce to the demand; it was a constant hunt for the money to buy what they needed.

But the business was solid, the beer was solid, and the future looked good. "We looked at the macro forces acting on the industry, and they're great," he said. "Craft beer is a long-term opportunity. The consumers are wising up to quality, they're appreciating finer beer. They won't go back."

The new owners want to improve things, but they don't plan huge shifts in the focus of the brewery. "We're changing things, but we're not rocking the boat," said Chris. "We want to drive the business forward, elevate the products and their perception, but we're not going to leave what we already have behind. We're not 'aged in oak barrels for $100 a case' guys. We make good beer; we don't want to change that."

"You'll see some more exciting products," Glenn amplified, "but you won't see us destroying our roots." What sounds like a "tweak but not twitch" philosophy saw early promise in a trial product they let me sample. Christian Ryan, who was brought in direct from a brewing degree program at UC Davis, has been working on creating a bottle-conditioned version of Belgian Freeze. It was still young, but it was noticeably drier, with a more intense yeast character. All smiles as we sampled it, and I'd put that down as promising. Christian and Tim Bryan, who's still brewing here as well, are also working on formulating two new seasonals for spring and fall.

"We want to be known for reliably good-quality beer," said Glenn, looking past the prologue, "a local brewery with consistently high-quality beer, and a higher energy level than it's had in the past. We're getting out in the community already; we're friendly. We're trying."

I hope it works. I'd like to see River Horse beers more often on the taps round about my home. Drop in and see how things are working out.

Opened: April 1996.

Owners: Glenn Bernabeo, Chris Walsh.

Brewers: Tim Bryan, Christian Ryan.

System: 25-barrel JV Northwest system, annual capacity 6,500 barrels.

Production: Approximately 4,500 barrels in 2006.

Tours: Gift shop open and tours available seven days a week, noon to 5 P.M.

Take-out beer: Two six-packs per person per visit, state maximum.

Extras: River Horse hosts several events during the year, including an Oktoberfest on-site. The brewery's beloved Chili Cook-Off during Lambertville's Winterfest in February and the big music jam during the Shad Festival in mid-April are still on but have moved off-site; check the River Horse website for details on dates and locations.

Special considerations: Kids welcome. Handicapped-accessible.

Parking: On-site lot.

Lodging in the area: Lambertville House, 32 Bridge Street, 609-397-0200; Lambertville Station, 11 Bridge Street, 609-397-4400; Chimney Hill Farm Inn, 207 Goat Hill Road, 609-397-1516.

Area attractions: Lambertville has plenty of attractions: a variety of restaurants, bars, and a plethora of antique shops. You can't really go wrong, but I'd like to point out a couple special places. First, **Mitchell's** (11½ Church Street, 609-397-9853) is a bar that does an Irish-Celtic jam session every first and third Wednesday of the month, and it's well worth attending. If you're looking for a nice piece of estate jewelry, **Park Place** (6 Bridge Street, 609-397-0102) has supplied a few happy smiles in my house. Then there's the **Shad Festival,** which takes over the town for a weekend every April (check the town's website, www.lambertville.org, for the date), with art, music, and food, including shad chowder, shad sausage, shad roe, and shad sandwiches. I love the silvery fish; it's one of my rituals for spring. Even if you don't like fish, go, have a good time, and sample some River Horse. **New Hope** is right across the river, an easy walk over the bridge, with even more shops and restaurants and some of the best people-watching around. There are bike trails on both sides of the river; the Jersey side is better at this point on the Delaware.

Other area beer sites: For years, the **Inn of the Hawke** (74 South Union Avenue, Lambertville, 609-397-9555) has been the only place for beer variety for miles around. Things have gotten better, beerwise, but the Hawke is still a prime option. Sipping a cool beer out back in the garden, under the shade of the spreading trees, is a longtime tradition for my wife and me. I used to say the best place for a beer in New Hope was to cross the bridge to Lambertville and go to the Inn of the Hawke, but **Triumph** cost me a good line. Their New Hope brewpub (400 Union Square Drive, 215-862-8300) not only sports great, multiple GABF award-winning beers, but the food's up to high New Hope standards, and it's an easy walk up the hill from the bridge, just across the New Hope and Ivyland Railroad tracks. For take-home, the best place in town is **Walker's Wines and Spirits** (86 Bridge Street, Lambertville, 609-397-0625), a decent beer selection, friendly help, and a nice old building to keep it all in.

The Ship Inn

61 Bridge Street, Milford, NJ
908-995-0188
www.shipinn.com

I was thinking about the times I've been to the Ship over the last ten years, and two things came to mind. First, it has been way too few times, considering it's a beautiful drive and less than an hour away. Second, I was amused to realize how many of them have been prefaced by my saying to my wife, "You know, hon, we're actually not too far from the Ship Inn." (If you're curious, 50 miles qualifies as "actually not too far.") I'm surprised she's never caught on; or maybe she likes the place as much as I do.

What's not to like! The Ship is my kind of brewpub. The building dates from the 1860s, and you can feel that in the openness of the room, the solid construction. It was a bakery, then an ice cream parlor (with a Prohibition-era speakeasy in the rear). Capping the whole feel of re-purposing, the surface of the bar is wood from two bowling lanes used in the town in the 1950s. I like old buildings made over into brewpubs.

I also like menus with a distinctive regionalism to them, not a menu that could be on any upscale chain restaurant. The food here is the English food of the owners (David Hall's from Hereford, Ann is an American who was raised in Liverpool), and it goes beyond the standard fish and chips, Scotch eggs, and bangers and mash you'll find in most wannabe pubs: sausage rolls, real roast beef and Yorkshire pudding, Lancashire cheese and onion pie, Tiddy Oggie (a kind of pasty, and if you don't know what a pasty is, just give up and go to Milford and order one), and the array of curries that have become as much a British staple as the Indonesian *rijstaafel* is a Dutch standard.

But most of all, I like cask ale, done right, and Tim Hall doesn't know how to do it any other way. "We do English beer," he said. "Our beers are brewed to be cask ales, and any excess carbonation is only there to appease the customer."

Tim will even fill growlers with cask ale and seemed disappointed when I told him I didn't know

Beers brewed: Year-round: ESB, Best Bitter, Golden Wheat, Porter. Seasonals and occasionals: Session Ale, Peculier Porter, Old Panhead Porter, Dark Charger Brown Ale, Pheasant Plucker Brown Ale, IPA.

of any other brewpub that would do that. "Of course we'll put cask ale in a growler," he said. "It's intrinsic to our identity. We do Yorkshire pudding, we do cask ale. It's all about consumer education, and cask-conditioned ale is the end point of that process. It's taken a long time, but we've reached a point of success where we have to keep at least one cask ale on all the time. The customers demand it."

If you don't know what cask ale is, a quick education is in order. Cask ale, or "real ale," is how all beers used to be consumed: right from the barrel, unfiltered and "alive." The brewery fills the cask with uncarbonated, unfiltered beer straight from the tanks, with the live yeast still in it. They may dose it with a small amount of sugar or fresh wort, and then they hammer home the bung to seal the cask. The beer will come to peak condition in the cask as it waits at the tavern.

The Pick: Mostly, it's whatever's on cask. These beers were made—were *bred*— for dispense as real ale, and that's how they truly shine. I took home a small beer-in-a-box full of ESB that Tim pulled off the tank for me, and it came to perfection at my house. I loved it: mild carbonation, a great estery, fruity aroma, and a malty just-sweet medium body that begged me to have another. So I did.

By the time the beer is tapped, it is lightly carbonated by a secondary fermentation done by the still-live yeast, fueled by the addition of sugar or wort. The cask has been sitting quietly, giving the yeast a chance to drop to the bottom. An ideal tapping will produce a clear glass of cellar-temperature (about 55 degrees Fahrenheit), lightly carbonated ale that has a fresh, estery aroma and flavor that cannot be matched by any other method of dispense.

When Ann Hall found out that New Jersey law was changing to allow in-house brewing, she knew that was what she wanted in the English tea-shop restaurant she'd opened in 1985, and she wanted to be the first legal brewpub in modern times in New Jersey, for the marketing value. They went to the man who was putting English ale breweries in places up and down the East Coast, Alan Pugsley, who was then working for an Englishman named Peter Austin. Austin had a brewery plan and a classic Yorkshire yeast strain called Ringwood.

Some beer geeks flat-out despise Ringwood-brewed beers for their distinctive nutty, buttery character. Some brewers think that Pugsley's and Austin's insistence on manual controls and open fermenters is backward in the twenty-first century. I asked Tim what he thought about opinions like that—or at least, I tried to, but he cut right into the question.

"I don't care about the beer geeks," he said. "Ringwood is reliable, and we have a good working relationship. What's wrong with a yeast that imparts flavor? It's core to this type of beer. You work with Ringwood and it becomes your yeast, it fits to your house.

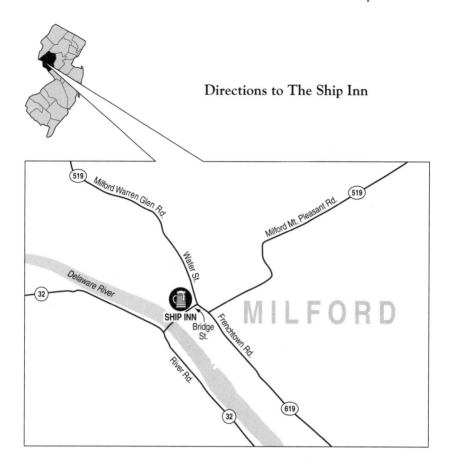

Directions to The Ship Inn

"It's like the water," he said, gesturing out the window at Milford Creek, and by extension, the Delaware River running a block away. "That's the water I've got, and I'm going to make the beer it lets me make. It's a bit Zen, but you've got to make the beer you've got."

He moved on to another point in what was becoming a beer manifesto, playing preacher to my amen corner: session beer, the idea of lower-alcohol beer with good flavor that can be drunk in longer "sessions" without leaving the drinker inebriated. "We just put out a beer called Session Ale," he said. "It's a reaction against American craft brewers equating more alcohol with more flavor. I find it overpowering, and the economics involved don't make sense either: People can't drink as much of it and won't buy as much of it!"

Solid stuff, and well reasoned, kind of what you'd expect from a brewer who teaches linguistics at Columbia University—brewing's a part-time job for Tim while he finishes his doctorate, although you can tell he suspects he'll still be brewing for mom and dad even after he's Dr. Hall. That sits a bit better with him than it did at the start.

"When we first opened," he recalled with a grin, "we had to develop a local business, and at first it was all older people. I was a lonely, lonely young single brewer. We have a younger crowd now that comes from as far as an hour, ninety minutes away: English sports-car enthusiasts, bikers, cyclists. It's taken a while, but we've got a good base now."

An hour away? See, it's like I told my wife: You're actually not that far from the Ship Inn. Could be time for a session this weekend.

Opened: Restaurant opened in May 1985; brewery opened January 3, 1995, as New Jersey's first post-Prohibition brewpub.

Owners: David and Ann Hall, Tim Hall, Christopher Hall, Heather Hall.

Brewer: Tim Hall.

System: 7-barrel Peter Austin system, 520 barrels annual capacity.

Production: Approximately 365 barrels in 2006.

Brewpub hours: Monday to Thursday, noon to 11 P.M.; Friday and Saturday, noon to midnight; Sunday, noon to 10 P.M.

Tours: Group tours by appointment, please. Informal individual tours available on request; ask your server.

Take-out beer: Half-gallon growlers and two sizes of beer-in-a-box (plastic bags with dispenser spigots): 5 quarts and 2.5 gallons. The Ship Inn will sell cask beer to go, unlike most brewpubs.

Food: The fare consists of traditional British dishes like fish and chips, cheese and onion pie, shepherd's pie, toad in the hole, and Scotch eggs, as well as fresh seafood dishes, curries, and some quite nice vegetarian selections. Chef Lonnie Lippert—"a brave and hardy soul," says Tim—uses local, fresh, and organic meats and vegetables as much as possible.

Extras: The Ship Inn has a good selection of Scotch whiskies and other beers (mostly, but not all, British), and there's always a cider available. You'll find a dartboard ("We'll have to move that farther from the bar . . . ," Tim mused, noting some recent close calls) and one television that is never turned on, a way of making a statement about what should go on in proper taverns. The Ship has live music on Saturday nights and also hosts special events on Guy Fawkes Day, St. David's Day, Robert Burns Day, and St. George's Day (which happens to be Tim's birthday).

Special considerations: Kids welcome. Vegetarian meals available. Handicapped-accessible (side entrance off Honeysuckle Lane). Cigar smoking allowed outside in season.

Parking: On-street parking and a large town lot across the street by the creek.

Lodging in the area: Chestnut Hill on the Delaware, Church Street, Milford, 908-995 9761 (walking distance to the Ship); Bridgeton House, 525 River Road, Upper Black Eddy, PA, 610-982-5856 (walking distance; across the bridge); Golden Pheasant Inn, 763 River Road, Erwinna, PA, 610-294-9595.

Area attractions: Milford has some nice shops and makes a rewarding place to walk around. Tim suggests setting out early and hitting the **Lovin' Oven** (17 Bridge Street) for breakfast. One of the best things about Milford is the river, and I've loved driving along it ever since we moved to the area in 1991. Given the price of fuel, though, you might be better off pedaling your way along the Delaware and Raritan Canal towpath, a well-kept bike and footpath that offers quiet views of the river. You can drop down the path 4 miles or so to **Frenchtown** and shop . . . actually, you'd better bring the car. Frenchtown has antiques, bookstores, art galleries, clothing boutiques, and some good eats at the Race Street Café. Soak up that riverside ambience.

Other area beer sites: The Ship Inn used to be the only game in town, and it was a long way to any other beer variety. But now siblings Amy and Ed Coss have gotten into the beer game just up the road at the **Milford Oyster House** (92 Water Street, Milford, 908-995-9411), and Milford's got choices. (Tim Hall's happy to see it, by the way; it brings more people to Milford for beer.) The menu is heavy on fresh seafood, a combination of simple preparations and house-made dishes. Ed's the chef, and a beer lover, so he keeps a rotating selection of imports, seasonals, and "semilocal" beers like Victory, Flying Fish, Brooklyn, and Stoudt's. There's also a carefully chosen small set of bottles and a surprising array of spirits. As Tim Hall says, "Country life is not necessarily sitting in the woods with a can of Genny Cream." The **Warrenside Tavern** (511 Route 173, Bloomsbury, 908-479-4513) has been out there in the western reaches of New Jersey since 1924. When you sit at the old bar and look around the place, and think about the rolling hills and farms outside, you wonder just what it was like back then: dirt roads, farm wagons, kerosene lamps. Bet they didn't have the decent taps they do now, and I'm certain they didn't have the amazing bottle collection that they sport these days. Like almost everywhere I've gone in New Jersey, the bar food, pub grub, is delicious, and the service is quick and friendly. The Warrenside feels like an all-afternoon place; might have to try that some day.

Triumph Brewing Company

138 Nassau Street, Princeton, NJ 08542
609-924-7855
www.triumphbrewing.com

TRIUMPH
BREWING COMPANY

It's a long walk to Triumph . . . and that's after you've come in the front door. You'll walk down a long, dark-painted hallway till you finally come to the brewpub itself, which opens up before you in a three-floor vista backed by the glass-fronted brewhouse, an effect I've always referred to as the "Theater of Beer."

You'd think that tall glass wall would create a goldfish-bowl effect for brewer Tom Stevenson, but he says it's not so: "The customers don't really pay attention, except when I wash the windows. Brewing is not a spectator sport. 'Look, he's hooking up a hose; look, he's flipping a switch.'"

It may not be exciting, but the results are popular. Triumph has three brewpubs, this original operation in Princeton and two in Pennsylvania: one that opened in New Hope in May 2003 and one in Old City Philadelphia that just opened in April 2007. It also has four brewers: Stevenson, Patrick Jones in Old City, Brendan Anderson at New Hope, and Jay Misson, the director of brewing operations. Together they have more than forty-five years of solid brewing experience.

Founder Adam Rechnitz is an experienced brewer himself, so it's no surprise that the industry tradition that a brewpub is a restaurant first and a brewery second doesn't hold at Triumph. "To be honest, I'd as soon have opened a brewery," admitted Rechnitz. He initially planned to be doing the brewing, but as it has with so many other folks, the demands of ownership dragged him out of the brewhouse, and he's had to settle for keeping the company's focus firmly on the beer.

"I've tried to make the food good as well," he said, "but the thrust has always been for the beer. If I hadn't thought that the East wasn't ready for another microbrewery, I would have opened a brewery. The restaurant business is brutal. It's a terrible thing to say, isn't it: I wish my business was something else!"

Don't let that put you off. Dining at Triumph can be as casual as a stylishly presented cone of fresh-cut fries (a house specialty) and a burger at the bar, with a pint of your usual. But you can also have a feast of seared scallops with a roasted four-onion garnish and house-made corn pudding, vegan dumplings, or grilled chicken with bowtie pasta and a chipotle cream sauce.

I'm sure Adam would tell me I've got my priorities mixed up: Get back to the beer. Stevenson's been at the brewpub since before it opened, a horticulturist by day, homebrewer by night, who decided it was time for a change and lucked into the brewing position when Rechnitz got busy.

Coming from outside brewing gives him a different perspective; Misson calls Stevenson "our innovative brewer." He's the one responsible for the Coffee & Cream Stout, a blend of milk stout made with milk sugar and coffee stout made with beans from a local coffee shop; Jewish Rye Beer, with caraway seeds, of course; and his throwback beer, Gothic Ale, a re-creation of the beers that were made with herbal mixtures before the use of hops.

"We have our three standard ales," Stevenson explained. "I try to have a stout of some kind and a lager on, and something on the beer engine [handpump], which leaves one tap for a seasonal, a wild card. I don't make those beers all that often, because I don't want their novelty to get worn out. I think of them as creative efforts that are in many cases delicious and very drinkable. But because they're not for everyone, we have to be a little careful about how often we make them."

What really sets Triumph apart is an attention to detail. It shows in the architecture, in the high-tech draft system Misson put together himself in Old City, in the "beer board" that shows what beers are in the tanks and when they'll be ready. It shows in the rigorous training the serving staff goes through, until they understand and can explain the difference between Triumph's German pilsner and the Czech pilsner—subtle, but real, and important to folks like you and me.

It even shows in the new glasses at all three pubs, swervy, curvy hand-comfortable glasses that look a lot like the one on the Triumph

Beers brewed: Year-round: Honey Wheat Ale, Amber Ale, Bengal Gold India Pale Ale. Seasonals and occasionals: Czech Pilsner (GABF Silver, 2005), Rauchbier (GABF Silver, 2004), Abbey Trippel, American Lager, Barleywine, Bock, Buckwheat Beer, Coffee & Cream Stout, Eisbier, Esteemed Beer, Extra Special Bitter, Gothic Ale, Hefe-Weizen, Helles Lager, Honey Wheat, Honeymoon Braggot, Ich Bin Ein Berliner Weisse, Imperial Stout, IPX, Irish Dry Stout, Irish Red Ale, Jewish Rye Beer, Jolie Blonde, Kölsch, Küchengerächertbier, Luftbier, Maerzen/Oktoberfest, Maibock, Mild Ale, Milk Stout, Munich Dunkel, Nut Brown Ale, Oatmeal Stout, Pale Ale, Poor Richard's Ale, Porter, Pumpkin Ale, Schwarzbier, Scottish Ale, Small Triumph Coffee Stout, Sour-Mash Raspberry Wheat, Special Bitter, Vienna Lager, Winter Wonder . . . and they probably missed a few.

logo. "We got these from Germany," Misson told me proudly. "They have a branding association, but they also feel good in the hand, and it's a traditional design. All the little things do add up. There's extra care in every level of this operation."

All the little things do add up. When you get a curvy glass of Bengal Gold IPA—if you take your time and sip it for full enjoyment—you can almost taste every one of them. And that's a triumph.

The Pick: For everyday drinking, I don't even have to think: The Bengal IPA is the beer I drink almost every time I go to Triumph. It's as good as you'd expect a beer to be after a guy's been making it for more than ten years: focused, balanced, hop-forward but not a tongue-ripper, and beautifully drinkable. For fun? I have the Coffee & Cream Stout whenever I see it. It's just crazy how much this beer tastes like its name.

Opened: March 14, 1995.

Owners: Adam Rechnitz, Brian Fitting.

Brewer: Tom Stevenson.

System: 10-barrel Newlands Systems Inc. system, potential annual capacity of 2,000 barrels.

Production: 1,330 barrels in 2006.

Brewpub hours: Monday to Saturday, 11:30 A.M. to 1 A.M.; Sunday, noon to midnight.

Tours: By appointment.

Take-out beer: Half-gallon growlers, quarter- and half-barrel kegs.

Food: Contemporary American cuisine is how they describe it; I just say it's imaginative. The vegetarian dishes are particularly good, and the seafood is handled with a deft touch. Be sure to get one of the cones of fresh-cut potato chips, a Triumph classic.

Extras: Live music on the weekends. Extensive single-malt and single-barrel bourbon lists.

Special considerations: Kids welcome. Vegetarian meals. Handicapped-accessible.

Parking: There's some limited on-street parking, but Triumph suggests visiting www.princetonparking.org for parking solutions.

Lodging in the area: Nassau Inn, 10 Palmer Square East, Princeton, 609-921-7500; Inn at Glencairn, 3301 Lawrenceville Road, Princeton, 609-497-1737; Hampton Inn, 4385 U.S. Highway 1, Princeton, 609-951-0066.

Area attractions: See suggestions for Princeton and Trenton in chapter introduction.

Other area beer sites: The *Alchemist and Barrister* (28 Witherspoon Street, Princeton, 609-924-5555) was where I used to have to go for a better beer selection when I first moved to southeastern Pennsylvania back in 1991. It was the place to go for a good beer or whisky in a pubby, clubby atmosphere, and it still is, a Princeton

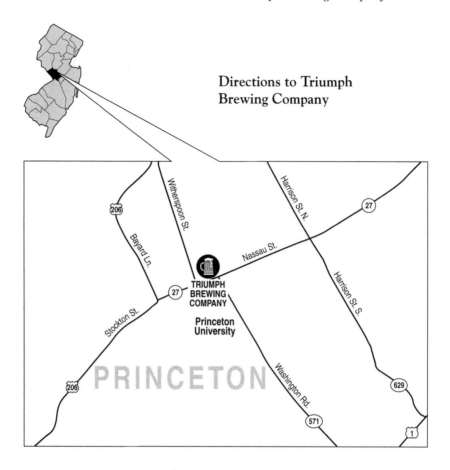

Directions to Triumph
Brewing Company

institution. The **Mill Hill Saloon and Eatery** (300 South Broad Street, just up the hill from the "Trenton Makes" bridge in Trenton (609-394-7222) would have been an entry in this book if we'd done it ten years ago; it used to have a small brewpub downstairs. But the license didn't transfer with the sale—another strange law—and now the Mill Hill just has the best corner-bar beer selection in Trenton; one of the best beer selections in South Jersey, actually. The food is solid home cooking with some flair to it; be sure to check the daily specials. The Mill Hill has that righteous feel you find in authentic neighborhood joints; make yourself a regular for a day.

Flying Fish Brewing Company

1940 Olney Avenue, Cherry Hill, NJ 08003
856-489-0061
www.FlyingFish.com

Gene Muller's running the second-biggest brewery in New Jersey. He's looking at real estate for a future expansion. When I visited, he had just bought a new, faster bottling line he was going to shoehorn into the current building. He does promotional events, like dinners and tastings. Gene's even done some lobbying for the brewers of New Jersey. What he doesn't do is brew. He's got head brewer Casey Hughes and his crew to do that.

"I was a writer, in advertising," he said, taking a break from doing everything but brewing. "I had traveled in the West and had good beer. I'd been homebrewing since the 1980s, and I started thinking about how it could work here. I wanted to open a brewpub in Old City Philadelphia. But the real estate was expensive, and I had no assets, no experience."

Then the lightbulb flashed as Gene was watching an Eagles game. "They had a shot of South Jersey from the Goodyear blimp as it was flying over Veterans Stadium," he said, "and I thought, 'Hey! I bet I could afford it there!'"

Sure enough, Gene had soon hooked up with a sympathetic landlord and was ready to get rolling. He lined up money, he started branding (that advertising experience would come in handy again and again), he went to the Siebel Institute to learn commercial-scale brewing. "Then I realized, someone's got to run the business," he said, a wry grin on his face. "In twelve years, I've done everything but brew."

He's lucky; a lot of guys back then would have done a lot better to have been as smart as Gene and paid more attention to running the business. Flying Fish got a head start by getting on the Web

Beers brewed: Year-round: Flying Fish Extra Pale Ale, Belgian Abbey Dubbel, Hopfish IPA, ESB Ale. Seasonals: Oktoberfish, Farmhouse Summer Ale, Grand Cru Winter Reserve. Occasionals and one-offs: Imperial Espresso Porter, Puckerfish sour ale, Big Fish Barleywine, Lovefish cherry ale (small batches of draft-only, for Valentine's Day), some draft-only small batches of bourbon barrel–aged Big Fish. Upcoming: Exit Series of small-batch big beers: Belgian styles, double IPA, Imperial stout, and the like.

in 1995; they were going to build their brewery on the World Wide Web. That's what everyone called it then; we weren't up to the point of just calling it the Web.

"The Yahoo! guys were still in college," said Gene. "It was real early for the Web. When a reporter from the *Philadelphia Inquirer* came to do a story on this guy who was putting a brewery on the Web, he had to come to my house to see the site on my computer; he didn't have a Web browser on his computer at work."

The "building the brewery on the Web" was a huge help, Gene told me. "We got a lot of media attention for it. It was all about the brand."

Why Flying Fish? Where did that catchy bony fish with the propellers come from? "The name came first," Gene said. "We had a list we came up with; it had about a thousand names. I just took a shot and sent some bottles of beer with no logo on them to Pentagram Design in New York, just this fabulous design firm. They got excited, liked the

Flying Fish name, and did it for cost." One of the benefits of being early on the beer scene, if you're taking notes.

One of the problems with being early on the beer scene was 1996, when things went flat. "We started sales in September 1996," Gene explained, "right when the bubble burst. Little guys were shipping beer everywhere, and no one had a lab, and a lot of beer went bad." It was tough for a while—the business wasn't profitable until 1999—but Gene and the company hung in there.

One of the things that set the tone for the company's success was staying local. "We sell most of the beer within 100 miles of this room," Gene said. "We sell in eastern Pennsylvania, Maryland, and Delaware, but 85 percent of our sales are in South Jersey and the five-county area" of southeastern Pennsylvania. "We want to be intensely local. The beer stays fresh, and with gas prices the way they are, it makes sense to stay local. And I think that as people get more sophisticated, they want local products. That's a good thing."

Another thing that has always been Flying Fish is the beer-food connection. "We were on the Belgian beer and beer-and-food thing years ago," said Gene, referencing the brewery's well-regarded Belgian Abbey Dubbel. "Beer dinners are great for introducing people to the fla-

Directions to Flying Fish Brewing Company

vors beer can have. We want to be food-friendly. You've got a restaurant with local food from local farmers? How about local beer?"

That ties into the third leg: drinkable beers. "When you sit down to a nice meal," Gene explained, "you don't want to overwhelm your palate with a huge beer. Flavor and texture have nothing to do with alcohol content. And lower alcohol percentages mean you can have another, and bars can sell another."

Has sticking to a few session-strength beers hurt Flying Fish with the beer aficionados? "Oh, yeah!" Gene said, and started laughing. "Just look at BeerAdvocate [a beer rating website]. I had to tell Casey to stop looking at what they were saying!"

Gene laughed again and recalled something said by Tom Baker, who ran Heavyweight Brewing, a small New Jersey brewery that did a lot of small-batch beers: "People always tasted my new beers and said, 'This is great! What's next?'"

"You're like a hamster on a wheel if you try to keep people like that happy," Gene told me. "You won't make payroll. You and me, the fans, we're always about what's new, what's different. I admit that. But it's about selling beer people will buy every day."

After twelve years, Gene's still busy, but he's got more perspective. "We're in a good position right now, making good money and not spending much. But it would be great to have more production breweries. Guys in some other states get support from the government. The wineries in New Jersey come under the Agriculture Department; they get everything!"

Hey, he's not whining, though. That's not likely from a guy who's just come up with the new slogan: "Proudly brewed in New Jersey. You got a problem with that?" Flying Fish is finally playing the Jersey card, and it's working; maybe it's a *Sopranos* effect. Gene and Casey are plotting an Exit Series of beers, with a new limited-release beer named for each exit on the New Jersey Turnpike. "I always liked Imperial stout," Gene said. "We're finally going to brew one. We're going to have some fun."

"Is it fun?" I asked him. The guy who does everything but brew sat back and thought about things. "No business is easy," he said. "But . . . I'm usually the last one out the door, and it is nice to have your own beer. It's a fun industry."

Spoken like a guy who's got a whimsical propeller-driven flying fish logo on his own beer. Gene Muller may not brew, but he's made a lot of good, drinkable, food-friendly beer in the past eleven years. It sounds as though he's just getting warmed up.

Opened: April 1995; production started August 1996.
Owner: Gene Muller.
Brewer: Casey Hughes.
System: 20-barrel Liquid Assets brewhouse, 13,000 barrels annual capacity.
Production: Approximately 10,000 barrels in 2006.
Tours: Saturdays, 1 P.M. to 4 P.M.
Take-out beer: Two six-packs per person per visit, state maximum.
Special considerations: Kids welcome. Handicapped-accessible.
Parking: On-site lot.
Lodging in the area: Days Inn, 525 State Route 38, Cherry Hill, 856-663-0100; Extended Stay America, 1653 Marlton Pike, Cherry Hill, 856-

616-1200; Residence Inn by Marriott, 1821 Old Cuthbert Road, Cherry Hill, 856-429-6111.

Area attractions: It's shoe madness at the **JDR Shoe Warehouse** (16 Springdale Road, Cherry Hill, 856-751-6668), just across the road from the brewery, with forty-five thousand pairs of shoes to choose from. That's Mom taken care of, now get the kids occupied at the **Garden State Discovery Museum** (2040 Springdale Road, Suite 100, Cherry Hill, 856-424-1233, www.discoverymuseum.com), with hands-on learning and fun activities that will have them excited and moving. If the brewery tour wasn't enough fun for Dad, bring out the big guns: The **Battleship New Jersey** is not far away, on the Camden waterfront (1 Riverside Drive, 866-877-6262, www.battle shipnewjersey.org). (That's the PSE&G garage, on the dock where the ship's moored.) You can tour BB-62 and see the big 16-inch guns that fired in combat over a span of more than forty years. You can combine your battleship tour with something a bit more pacific: The **Adventure Aquarium** (1 Aquarium Drive, Camden, 856-365-3300, www.adventureaquarium.com) is nearby and offers a combined ticket with the battleship. Penguins, sharks, rays, seals, and even hippos—all in Camden. If that's not enough, **Philadelphia** is just across the bridge (pick a bridge, any bridge), with all that shopping, and history, and art—and beer. Just keep in mind that if it comes down to a rumble, the smart money's on the *New Jersey* against Philadelphia's Spanish American War–era battlewagon, the *Olympia!*

Other area beer sites: Philadelphia may be better known for its gastropubs, but South Jersey has its very own: **Cork** (90 Haddon Avenue, Collingswood, 856-833-9800). This chic bistro may not look like much from its storefront exterior, but the inside is high-design, and the tap selection is the best in South Jersey, maybe the best in the state for its size. The spirits and wine are equally well picked, and the food is adventurous and deftly prepared. Time for a night out. There's a seat at the bar waiting for you at **Brewer's Towne Tavern** (Crystal Lake and Haddon Avenues, Westmont, 856-854-5545), a nice, unpretentious corner bar with some local taps. It's clean, you've got flat-screens, pool tables, and tattoos, and the folks have been friendly whenever I've dropped in. If you're in the area, you'll find something worth your time here. There are two **P. J. Whelihan's** nearby (700 North Haddon Avenue, Haddonfield, 856-427-7888, and 1854 East Marlton Pike, Cherry Hill, 856-424-8844), representatives of a midsize regional chain of beer-oriented casual restaurants. The beer selection isn't quite as good as it was in the early years, but you'll still find some local crafts, PJ's Copper Lager, and some bigger crafts and imports. Okay, **Pietro's** (140 West Route 70, Evesham, 856-596-5500, just off the infamous Marlton Circle, right beside Olga's Diner) isn't really a bar, and the beer's only a little better than average—a cut above the usual macrobrewed offerings you'll find around here, with some imports and big crafts—but you're here for the pizza, which is baked in coal-fired ovens and topped with delicious stuff (prosciutto and caramelized Bermuda onions will not do you wrong, my friends). Get a pie and a pint, and you'll see my wisdom.

A word about . . .

New Jersey Food

W hen you think about New Jersey and food, what should come to mind is a bounty. It's not called the Garden State for nothing, you know. The state with the highest population density is also a leading producer of fruits and vegetables: second in the nation in production of blueberries and potatoes, and third in cranberries. Peaches have outstripped the apple production that once made the ice-distilled applejack known as Jersey lightning revered and feared throughout the colonies.

Most locals know two things about New Jersey agriculture: tomatoes and sweet corn. I was raised to believe that Pennsylvania produce was superior—to everything—but even I have to admit that the big, juicy tomatoes and sweet, crisp corn we're getting out of New Jersey are delicious stuff. My family has been part of a New Jersey–based organic community-supported agriculture (CSA) program offered at Honey Brook Organic Farm in Pennington (www.honeybrookorganicfarm.com) for three years. We get a box of produce each week from April to early November. I've never enjoyed radishes so much, and the strawberries are the tastiest I've ever had. Hats off to New Jersey produce!

But hey . . . who really thinks about all that healthy stuff when you're talking serious food? I'd rather have a beer with a big plate of baked ziti than a big plate of blueberries, y'know what I'm talking about? Let's talk about the stuff New Jersey's really known for, serious chowing down. This state has more diners than any other, as many as six hundred. If you want to find one wherever you are in the state, fire up the Web and hit www.NJDiners.com, some folks who know diners.

What do you get at the diner? The classic New Jersey meal-in-a-hand is pork roll with egg and cheese on a hard roll, or maybe a bagel. Unless you call it a Taylor Ham with egg and cheese, which about half the state does.

Pork roll is a very Jersey thing, invented and still made in Trenton by the Taylor Provisions Company and sold as John Taylor's Pork Roll. (And before the arguments start about the "real name" of the product or the company—as they will, this is passionate stuff—I'm taking that right from the wrapper of my latest chunk of pork roll. I'm looking at it *right now*, okay?) John Taylor, the original John Taylor, a New Jersey state senator, first made pork roll in 1856. It still comes in a sewn cloth wrapper, like a real sausage, not a "formed meat product."

Don't ask about the recipe or ingredients. It's a held-to-the-death secret. The wrapper has only this: "Pork, salt, sugar, spices, lactic acid starter culture, sodium nitrite, sodium nitrate." Classic cured sausage, in other words. Think Spam, but pork roll is leaner, has a hint of smoke, subtly different spices—and it doesn't have the goo or come in a can.

You'll notice I keep calling it "pork roll." Most of you won't find that odd, but those of you in North Jersey are shaking your heads. "Dumb Pennsy boy," you're thinking. "It's Taylor ham, not pork roll." The state splits just about across the middle on this, north and south. The north calls it "Taylor ham" and eats it with mustard; the south calls it "pork roll" and eats it with ketchup. Over here in the Philadelphia area, the only place outside of New Jersey you can be sure of finding pork roll (my local market carries five different brands), it's pork roll; hey, Trenton's right across the river, and that's what it says on the wrap!

Get down to it: Let's eat some and stop arguing. Better than three-quarters of the pork roll sold is consumed in some variation of the pork roll, egg, and cheese sandwich mentioned above. The New Hope, Pennsylvania, based band Ween has a song called "Pork Roll, Egg, and Cheese." It's an icon. I just fried one up (strictly in the name of research, of course): Slice the pork roll, notch it around the rim in four places, and throw it in the hot skillet. You don't need to grease the pan; the pork roll is self-lubricating!

As the pork roll cooks, it shrinks, which is why you notch it; otherwise you wind up with cupped slices of meat that aren't crispy all over. The properly notched meat will look like a Maltese cross when you're done. Throw an egg in there (you can go scrambled or over easy, depending on the diner), and then melt some American cheese on your hard roll (not really "hard"; this is just another name for a kaiser or club roll). Then it's SPK time: salt, pepper, and ketchup . . . or mustard, I suppose, if you're in North Jersey. There you have it, smelling great, looking fine, a classic New Jersey breakfast.

Natives are often crushed to find that pork roll doesn't make it far out of the state. There are a number of mail-order pork roll suppliers that have sprung up to supply their addiction; Google "pork roll" and you'll find all of them, I guarantee. One thing: If you do get a mail-order pork roll, eat it all within a couple days. Contrary to what some might tell you, it doesn't freeze well. Get some friends and introduce them to pork roll, eat it all up: PRE&C, SPK!

Whew. I feel like a little dessert after all that pork roll. How about a piece of saltwater taffy? Everyone comes home from the shore with a box of this sweet, chewy stuff; it's how you know someone was "down the shore." It was invented—or first marketed—in Atlantic City in the late 1800s. Taffy has been around for a long time, but this stuff was pulled and pulled and pulled . . . and for reasons not completely clear, was also called "saltwater" taffy.

It became popular, and just as fudge is the confection people bring home from Lake Michigan shore towns, saltwater taffy was what you had when you were in Atlantic City. It is part of the Boardwalk experience, a 1-pound cardboard box full of multicolored chunks of taffy, wrapped in waxed paper. I've never been much of a taffy guy, but I can remember the texture, the smooth glossy surface, and the sweet melting flavor. I also remember my teeth being stuck together and thinking I'd lose some before I got my mouth open again, which is why I've never been much of a taffy guy!

Rippers are much easier to chew. They should be; they're deep-fried hot dogs. The place to get them, the original, is Rutt's Hut in Clifton (417 River Road, 973-779-8615). They've been doing hot dogs in hot fat there since 1928. And they're not all called "rippers." A ripper is just one degree of doneness, in which the dog's cooked till the skin rips open. You can also get an in-and-outer, which is put in the frier for just a quick bath, or a cremator, which gets pretty black and crispy.

Don't let me tell you what to do, but listen: You want the ripper. Why? It's the best balance between crisp and soft, the edges of the ripped skin get really flavorful, and the openings let the meat juices out to mingle with the special house mustard relish. It's not really something you can do right at home—special hot dogs, special relish, and precise temperature on the deep frier—so you'll just have to get to Clifton.

There's lots of other good stuff in New Jersey and things they do in the Garden State like nowhere else. We could get into a battle royal over pizza alone, and there's a whole subculture of Italian restaurants. And then there's the somewhat secretive M&M–Mars compound in Hackettstown (yes, they do research and manufacturing there; no, you can't get a tour).

As I always say, though, this calls for more research. Hop in the car and go find a diner; you won't have to go far!

Skylands

The contrast could hardly be greater. Hoboken, Jersey City, Bayonne, and Secaucus run almost seamlessly into one another, dense blocks of houses and businesses clinging to the escarpment of the Palisades, looking across the busy waters of the Hudson River to the helicopter-buzzed hive of Manhattan. Jetliners roar overhead constantly, refinery flares and sodium vapor lamps light the night and hide the stars, and highways cover the earth, running over, above, and below it. People eat, laugh, work, love, and sleep in close proximity, enjoying that close proximity and the access it gives to everything they need.

But less than 50 miles away is High Point State Park, in the heart of the New Jersey Skylands. It's green and clean. Tall ridges roll across the countryside, west to the Delaware Water Gap National Recreation Area. Lakes stretch along the valleys. There are even ski slopes. You can see what New Jersey looked like before the advent of the automobile, out here where the superhighways don't run within spitting distance of each other.

Let's start in the west, along the Delaware, in the jewel that is the Delaware Water Gap. The river cuts a 900-foot-wide gash through the mountains here, and it's worth the trip just for the view alone. But there's so much more to do. The fishing is top-notch, and you'll see fly fishers working the streams. You can hike on a section of the Appalachian Trail, the Coppermine Trail, and the Highlands Trail, which is still being completed. Camping, mountain and road biking, canoeing and kayaking, golf, hot-air ballooning . . . there's so much to do here. For information on fishing in New Jersey, visit the Division of Fish and Wildlife's website, www.state.nj.us/dep/fgw/index.htm. For information on all the state parks and the activities they offer, visit the Division of Parks and Forestry's comprehensive website, www.state.nj.us/dep/parksandforests/.

Skiing is the thing in Vernon Valley—or rather, snowboarding is the thing. **Mountain Creek** (200 Route 94, 973-827-2000) has an Olympic-size half pipe and five terrain parks. If you're not traveling in the winter, pack your bike for some wicked downhill madness: In the summer, Mountain Creek turns into **Diablo Freeride Park,** a downhill bike park. Ride the chairlift up with your bike and blast down the mountain . . . and then do it all again (www.diablofreeridepark.com). If you remember Action Park in Vernon Valley—and God knows, I do—the scary old days of what was one of America's first water parks are over, and **Mountain Creek Waterpark** (www.mountaincreekwaterpark .com) is fun . . . and safe.

Unfortunately, Mountain Creek doesn't have a microbrewery like Action Park did, where Triumph's Jay Misson learned to brew old-school lagers. I got that beer twice—once at the park, where it was freezing cold and left me wondering what all the fuss was about, then again later at a tasting at the famous Brickskeller in Washington, D.C., where it was served properly and wowed me. A water park with a brewery—what a country.

What Vernon does have is a microdairy, if you will: **Bobolink Dairy** (42 Meadow Burn Road, 973-764-4888, www.cowsoutside.com) is a sustainable dairy farm, raising grass-fed cattle and whey-fed pork, making artisanal cheeses from that grass-fed milk, and baking fresh bread. You can go buy this good food (see the website for current hours). You also can take advantage of short internships in cheese- and breadmaking, or if you're looking for a career change (in a brewery book? That's where I found mine!), they offer longer apprenticeships as well. Oh, and they also make a cheese, their Bobolink-Foret, that's washed in Belgian ale. Pretty neat.

High Point State Park (www.state.nj.us/dep/parksandforests/parks/highpoint.html) is just what you'd expect: the highest point in New Jersey, 1,803 feet above sea level, with the High Point Monument rising another 220 feet above that. You can climb to the top (9 A.M. to 4:30 P.M. daily in the summer season, noon to 4 P.M. on weekends the rest of the year) for a panoramic view of the mountains of three states. There's swimming at Lake Marcia in the summer, and fishing too; just beware that Marcia is spring-fed, and she's a bit on the cold side. There's camping and hiking, and cross-country skiing in the winter.

Keep your eyes open: New Jersey is home to a black bear population that has been estimated at numbers as high as thirty-five hundred. More than half of them live in the Skylands. There have been two black bear hunting seasons, in 2003 and 2005, amid continued legal protests from environmentalists and animal-rights groups. Almost everyone agrees that the black bear population is a problem in the country's most densely populated state, but it's not clear what has to be done. You, of course, should view black bears from a safe distance and a bear-proof venue. Like a bar.

Get out into the Skylands, see the other side of New Jersey. Maybe it's the other side of Bayonne and Jersey City; maybe it's the other side of the Pine Barrens. Or maybe you want to see a whole other side of the Skylands: the top side. *Sky Sweeper Balloon Adventures* (just west of Clinton, 800-462-3201, www.skysweeper.com) will take you up high enough to get a great view of this beautiful area.

This is New Jersey too, which might give you a whole new perspective on the state.

High Point Brewing Company

22 Park Place, Butler, NJ 07405
973-838-7400
www.ramsteinbeer.com

"Traditional German beers made with American innovations is how I would describe them," explained Greg Zaccardi, owner and founder of High Point Brewing of Butler while we stood in the brewery tasting room enjoying a few samples. Here is a man who knows German beers firsthand and knows how he wants his beers to be.

After being initiated into the "Good Beer Club" while at the University of California–Santa Cruz, he returned to the East Coast to find nothing of interest. "When I returned, the most exotic thing I could find was Molson Golden. I realized that the only recourse was to learn to brew my own!"

Bitten by the homebrew bug and the love bug at about the same time was more than coincidence, it was kismet. His wife-to-be was a German *Fräulein*

Beers brewed: Year-round: Ramstein Blonde, Ramstein Classic, Ramstein Golden Lager. Seasonals and occasionals: Ramstein Winter Wheat, Ramstein Maibock, Ramstein Munich Amber Lager (Oktoberfest), Parnell Pale Ale.

whose family had longtime roots in the brewing industry back in the Old Country. His father-in-law found out Greg's interest in brewing and said, "*Komm herüber*" (Come over here)!

Before too long, Greg found himself with an apprenticeship in a Bavarian brewery, learning the traditional methods and styles that made Germany a beer heaven for centuries. Because of his already advanced knowledge of brewing, his stint at the brewery was accelerated. A year later, he returned to New Jersey ready to begin the conversion of the uninitiated to the world of real German wheat beers.

The Pick: Ramstein Winter Wheat is just awesome, a whopping beer, wobbling with flavor, yet drinkable and not cloying. Wait for it, and seize the day.

"I loved the beers of Germany, and I wanted to be able to share them with Americans who may never get the chance to travel there," Greg said. "I decided to make all wheat beers because it was an untapped market on the East Coast."

For those unfamiliar with brewing, wheat beers are not the easiest styles to brew. Wheat has a tendency to become sticky in the mash, and without proper equipment or preparation, the brewer can have a long day at the kettles. The custom system Greg had manufactured for the brewery helps immensely in this aspect.

Soon after his return, Greg began looking for a suitable location to set up his brewery. High Point was his first choice, as it emulated the Alpine foothills and forests he grew to love in Germany, but he settled on Butler, just a bit south of there, as the place to build his dream. It had water from a spring-fed reservoir and the industrial space needed to handle the equipment.

That was the birth of the High Point Wheat Beer Company. They chose the name Ramstein for the brand to show that German-American connection. Ramstein is a city in Germany that is home to Ramstein Air Base, a very large U.S. facility, and entertains a good-size American population.

His use of imported German and English grains and all noble hops gives High Point the quality Greg looks for in his products. He persuaded the small brewery in Bavaria to allow him to use their proprietary yeast strain for his own here in the United States. The yeast gives the beer that "special something" that sets it apart from the others.

"My vision was always to make beergarden-fresh beer for the Garden State," Greg said, "and I believe I've succeeded in that goal." It is no wonder that the brewery has garnered medals at TAP New York almost every year for its excellence in brewing.

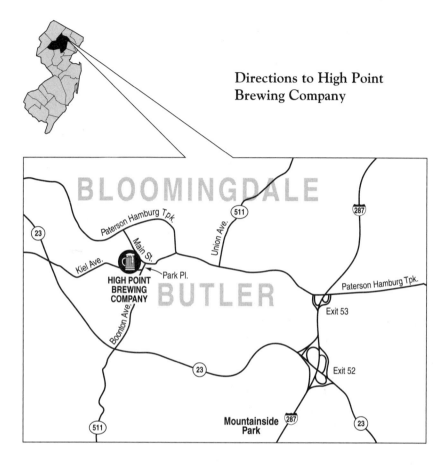

Directions to High Point
Brewing Company

He's decided to expand his repertoire a bit and, in the last few years, has brewed beers without wheat in the grist. Greg removed the "Wheat Beer" from the company name and became High Point Brewing Company. The Golden Lager is made with *pilsener* malt and noble hops to produce an exceptionally flavorful rendition of the beers we grew up with. His Parnell Pale Ale is brewed as a seasonal and is slightly different than most pales, as it is made with the German and English ingredients they always keep in-house.

"I'm always looking to impress people beyond their expectations when I introduce a new product to the lineup," revealed the owner. "I believe the tendency toward mediocrity in American brewing is ending, and once again quality and distinction are the watchwords."

This is proven by the meteoric growth this company has experienced in the last few years. His attention to detail and quality has paid off with distribution to some of the most prestigious restaurants in the Big Apple and North Jersey. "Our growth curve is going off the charts, and we've reached the top end of our capacity. Expansion of the brewery is now inevitable," Greg said. "Plans are to add more tank space as soon as possible, but even that has a limit with the square footage we occupy."

Greg is an outspoken advocate for New Jersey beers, but he sees a few changes that would certainly enhance the growth of the industry in the state. "You can go into a winery and buy as much as you want directly from the producer," he said, "but with beer, I can only sell two six-packs per person per visit. We need to get some legislative support in order to bring breweries and brewpubs into this new world. The arcane rules under which we operate make it difficult to stay here in New Jersey. With the hurdles they make you overcome, your business plan had better be the best or you'll be out very quickly."

The brewery holds an open house the second Saturday of every month from March to December. Greg found that the weather in January and February is just too unpredictable to have a reliable crowd. At these events, he fills growlers for his tap-only products and sells six-packs of his flagships, and he conducts tours for those interested.

It had been several years since we last visited, and the brewery has indeed grown. Some of the tanks have been moved in order to use the space more efficiently. They built a comfortable tasting room where the bar was once open to the brewery and display their medals and press accolades on the wall; a small wood-burning stove removes the chill from the space when Old Man Winter arrives. You can observe the activity in the brewhouse, yet remain separated from the noise and bustle.

Be sure to stop in at one of the open houses and visit with Greg and staff. It will certainly be the High Point of your day.

Opened: 1994.
Owner: Greg Zaccardi.
Brewer: Greg Zaccardi.
System: 15-barrel Criveller system, 4,000 barrels annual capacity.
Production: 3,200 barrels in 2006.
Tours: Second Saturday of each month, 2 P.M. to 4 P.M., except for January and February.
Take-out beer: Two six-packs per person per visit, state maximum.
Special considerations: Handicapped-accessible.
Parking: Parking lot in the industrial complex.

Lodging in the area: Butler Guest House, 68 Bartholdi Avenue, Butler, 973-492-0503; Roserne Motor Lodge, 23 High Street, Butler, 973-838-3434.

Area attractions: *Ringwood State Park* (1304 Sloatsburg Road, Ringwood, 973-962-7031) almost has it all: hiking, swimming, boating, bike trails (single-track mountain bike trails and less challenging stuff for guys like me), hunting, fishing. The **New Jersey Botanical Garden** (973-962-7527) is inside the park at the junction of Sloatsburg and Morris Roads, formal gardens with a focus on flowering trees. There are also two mansions inside the park: **Skylands Manor**, a Tudor Revival home at the center of the Botanical Garden, and **Ringwood Manor**, a Gothic Revival home just north of the Garden (www.ringwoodmanor.com).

Other area beer sites: What do you make of a bar dedicated to Jack Kerouac and great beer? ***The Shepherd and the Knucklehead*** (529 Belmont Avenue, Haledon, 973-790-9657) is not a big place, and it's not easy to find, but its beer selection is one of the top five in the state. The bar's about the size of a large living room and might hold thirty-five people—and chances are that if it did, they'd all be talking. This is one we're going to have to tell you to experience on your own—and encourage you to do so!—because there's just no easy way to put it in words. It's a *gestalt* thing.

As Springsteen said, glory days, they'll pass you by. That's what happened at the **Front Porch** (217 Wagaraw Road, Hawthorne, 201-427-4331). Once upon a time, they had a big selection of beers and one of those "hall of foam"–type clubs you could get in if you drank all of them; the record sheets of past members are still kept in holders on the wall. There are still a few good taps and a couple of good bottles—any place with Spaten Optimator available can't be all bad—but it ain't what it used to be. Still worth a stop for food, a pint, and some memories.

I'd been driving past Boonton on I-287 for years, never knowing what a neat little town I was overlooking. Main Street is a winding corridor of shops and restaurants at the bottom of the steep hill on the northeast side of town, and the **Boonton Avenue Grill** (108 Boonton Avenue, Boonton, 973-316-9090) clings to the side of that hill. It's a sprawling place, with a broad menu—be sure to check the big board for the plentiful specials and seasonal additions—and a slightly better-than-average beer selection; you take what you can get sometimes, beerwise. Don't miss the watcher at the big window behind the bar; it's a fun trick to play on new visitors. There's another branch of **The Office** near here too (32 Chestnut Street, Ridgewood, 201-652-1070). You can get some take-out at these places: **Bottle King**, 476 Route 17 North, Ramsey, 201-934-9080; **Grand Opening Liquors**, 1068 High Mountain Road, North Haledon, 973-427-4477; **Ramsey Liquors**, 47 West Main Street, Ramsey, 201-327-0353.

Krogh's Restaurant and Brew Pub

23 White Deer Plaza, Sparta, NJ 07871
973-729-8428
www.kroghs.com

We set out early to make the long trek to this most out-of-the-way place. After traversing some of the most scenic areas in northwestern New Jersey, we finally arrived in the small town of Sparta . . . and proceeded to get lost. We had been here several years ago, but this time we depended on Web-generated directions that were not quite correct. Several phone calls later, we pulled up to the home of Krogh's Restaurant and Brew Pub.

As you stand in front of the building, you're transported back to a time of legend where edifices of this style existed. High-peaked roofs, Tudor battens, and stone facades conjure up visions of fairy tales and storybook characters. I almost expected to see the Seven Dwarfs come marching out of the entrance to greet us. Instead, the owner's wife, Barbara Fuchs, welcomed us at the door. The outside appearance definitely prepares you for the rustic interior: The hand-hewn beams, filled log walls, and log posts standing like trees sprouting out of the floor are from another century and belie the building's true age.

Speaking of age, let me take a moment to relate a bit of the area's history to help explain the evolution of the brewpub. Sparta was established back in 1845 as a very small community amid farms, open fields, mountains, and forests. Back in the early 1900s, the area known as Brogden Meadow was a large plot of 2,300 acres. In the early 1920s, the

Beers brewed: Year-round: Krogh's Gold, Alpine Glow Red Ale, Brogden Meadow Pale Ale, Log Cabin Nut Brown, Old Krogh Oatmeal Stout, Three Sisters Golden Wheat. Seasonals: Celebration Ale, Maibock, Honey Wheat, Octoberfest, Lindfors Lager.

Arthur D. Crane Company proceeded to buy up this land from some three hundred owners, then dammed the valley and flooded it from the Wallkill River, naming it Lake Mohawk. This put the heretofore unknown area on the map. The population increased significantly as the lakeside properties were developed and a tourist trade took root.

The Pick: Brogden Meadow Pale Ale is an assertively hopped selection with a pleasant citrus bite, but not over the top.

In 1927, a small tearoom and gift shop was opened, but after Prohibition ended, the owner decided to convert it into a tavern. The Carl Malmquist Restaurant flourished until 1937. That year, Frede Krogh purchased the property, renaming it Krogh's Restaurant and Tap Room. As Mrs. Krogh aged, and handling the cooking chores became impossible, a rough-and-tumble bar crowd took over. In 1973, Krogh's met its third owner, who reopened the kitchen.

In 1981, Bob Fuchs bought the property and set about making the restaurant a destination. Then, in 1999, he made Sussex County history by installing a brewery, making the restaurant the first brewpub in the county. "Bob wanted to open a restaurant and had been brewing at home, so the idea of a brewpub was born out of that," explained Barbara, Bob's wife. Nearly a decade has passed, and Krogh's still brews up the best beers and food around.

Making the trek to this location requires some driving from almost anywhere, so they know they have to be the best in order to remain in business. They depend on word-of-mouth recommendation to draw in new customers, and repeat business is crucial. "Sparta has become a year-round community, and we have acquired a loyal customer base from the residents," chimed in Dave Cooper, the brewer, who has been in the area for the last twenty-five years. "The area has grown so quickly from the commuters who wish to live in a country setting. But no longer do you see small lakeside cottages; rather, very large monuments to affluence."

Being a regular can have its rewards. Participating in Krogh's Frequent Diners Programs can get you free desserts, your name on a brass tag you may attach to the walls, or gift cards, including the Brew Club, Wine Club, Martini Club, Dessert Club, or For Kids Only Club.

The beer appellations derive from real people or places. "The Three Sisters Golden Wheat refers to Dave's three daughters," Barbara told me, "and they hate it! Being older now, they would prefer not to be immortalized like that." Alpine Glow Red Ale is named for the Alpine section of the lake, Log Cabin Nut Brown for the building that houses Krogh's, and Brogden Meadow Pale Ale for the original name of the area. There is even a Krogh still residing in town.

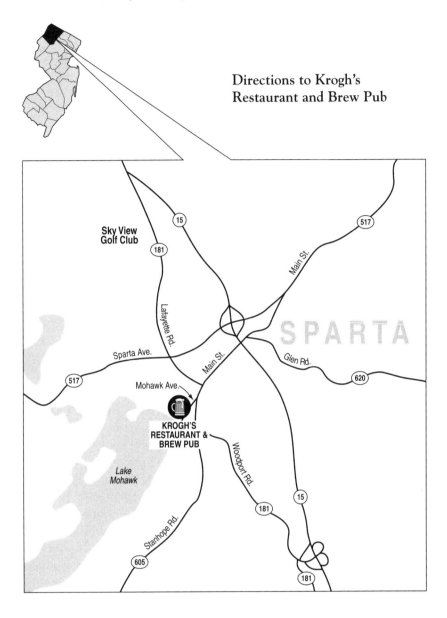

Directions to Krogh's Restaurant and Brew Pub

We got to taste them all in a sampler, and my favorite is the Brogden Meadow Pale Ale, the hoppiest of the group. The seasonal Octoberfest was great, but it's available for only a short time. It's all Dave can do to keep up with demand. Lagers and specialties are plan-ahead projects, as they take up fermenter space that could be used for more mainstream products.

For the past four years, the winner of the New Jersey State Fair homebrew competition has been able to assist Dave in brewing the winning style, which is then put on tap at the brewpub as a seasonal. "People really enjoy getting to try something totally different," said Dave. "We've had great success with the program. I made a Russian Imperial Stout one year but could only get a bit more than 3 barrels out of it because of the weight of the grist." One of those disadvantages of a small place!

Living in a small town makes public relations a very important phase of the business. "We sponsor charity events for many of the local organizations: Big Brothers and Big Sisters, the Red Cross, Juvenile Diabetes, and the Sparta Education Association," said Barbara. "The events are fun and make money for a good cause."

Next time you're sick of the traffic and congestion, point your vehicle toward Sparta and let its Waldenesque charm embrace you. Relax and have a beer and a meal while enjoying the ambience and the view. The owners and staff are proud of what they've accomplished here. They have a lot to Krogh about!

Opened: Opened as Krogh's Restaurant and Tap Room in 1937 and became Krogh's Restaurant and Brewpub in 1999.

Owner: Bob Fuchs.

Brewer: Dave Cooper.

System: 5-barrel DME system, 400 barrels annual capacity.

Production: 400 barrels in 2006.

Brewpub hours: Seven days a week, 11:30 A.M. to 2 A.M.

Tours: None offered.

Take-out beer: Half-gallon standard and deluxe growlers.

Food: A large menu with lots of offerings: appetizers, salads, sandwiches, fajitas, entrées, and an exceptional choice of desserts. To go along with these tasty morsels is a list of gourmet coffees.

Extras: All the entertainment is local talent. Acoustic music in the bar on Tuesdays, open-mike night on Thursdays, live music on Friday and Saturday, and food and drink specials every day. Fully stocked bar.

Special considerations: Kids welcome. Vegetarian meals available. Handicapped-accessible.

Parking: Street parking. Valet parking offered on Friday and Saturday nights.

Lodging in the area: Most visitors are lake rentals and owners, but there are a few B&Bs nearby where you can enjoy the country living. **Brick House Farm Bed and Breakfast** (125 Sparta Avenue, Sparta, 973-726-5713) has 7 acres of beautiful country vistas, with lots of activities, such as hiking, biking, and horseback riding nearby. **The Wooden Duck Bed and Breakfast** (140 Goodale Road, Newton, 973-300-0395)—how can you go wrong? Look at the address! **The Whistling Swan Inn** (110 Main Street, Stanhope, 973-347-6369) is near Allamuchy State Park and offers an exceptional breakfast.

Area attractions: Kittatinny Valley State Park near Andover has hiking, mountain biking, fishing, hunting, picnicking . . . all the things you do at a park and a bit more: Kittatinny also has dog-sledding trails. Mush, Fido! Check the Division of Parks and Forestry website (www.state.nj.us/dep/parksandforests/parks/kittval.html). Two museums recall the mining that took place in the area. **Sterling Hill Mine Museum** (30 Plant Street, Ogdensburg, 973-209-7212) is a tribute to one of two local mines where zinc ore was once extracted from the earth. **Franklin Mineral Museum** (32 Evans Street, Franklin, 973-827-3481; open April to November) is dedicated to rare fluorescent finds. There also are several golf courses: **Skyview Golf Club** (226 Lafayette Road, Sparta, 973-726-4653); **Rolling Greens Golf Club** (214 Newton-Sparta Road, Newton, 973-383-3082); and **Black Bear Golf and Country Club**, Route 23, Franklin, 973-209-2226).

Other area beer sites: It might look like just another gin joint along a divided highway in New Jersey, but once you grab the antler handle on the big wooden door at **The Thirsty Moose** (400 Route 15 South, Lake Hopatcong, 973-361-7600), you'll feel as though you walked into a backwoods bar in the Rocky Mountains. Okay, maybe more like the Catskills, but you get the idea. The taps are a definite improvement over the monoculture you'll see in most places in the area, and there's Moosehead, of course. The menu favors carnivores, with big steaks and buffalo burgers, and the prices are pretty reasonable. The **Mason Street Pub** (24 Mason Street, Lake Hopatcong, 973-663-4412) is a bit hard to find the first time—it's easier by boat—and the beer selection's nothing great, but the view of the lake is enough to convince you that a cold macrobrew every now and then is not all bad.

Once you've got your B&B reservations, pick up some refreshments for your stay at **White Deer Package Store** (4 White Deer Plaza, Sparta, 973-729-6025) or **Shoprite Liquors of Byram** (80-90 U.S. Highway 206, Stanhope, 973-448-9770).

Long Valley Pub and Brewery

1 Fairmount Road, Long Valley, NJ 07853
908-876-1122
www.longvalleypubandbrewery.com

New Jersey is a state of contrasts. The southern part is flat, sandy, and covered with scrub pine, while the north is mountainous, rocky, and covered with tall, stately pines and mighty oaks. Each has its charm, but for someone who was raised on the beaches at the Jersey Shore, the sight of the tree-draped mountains is always a treat. The scenic drive to this brewpub is surpassed only by the vistas before you when you arrive. Pull into the parking lot of Long Valley Pub and Brewery and the view couldn't be more picturesque. The massive Schooleys Mountain is the backdrop for this two-hundred-year-old barn converted into one of the most stunning restaurants you'll ever see.

Built by German immigrants in 1771 as a bank barn, its massive stone walls and hewn beams have largely passed the test of time. The renovations done in 1995 brought back the character of the original building, but it also needed to be augmented to be a viable restaurant and brewery location. As many of the original elements as could be saved were reintroduced into the renovations. The large beams were recycled into the second-floor loft, and laminated beams were installed where necessary for structural stability.

This makes a true blending of old and new . . . both in the brewery and in the building. Joe Saia, the brewer, has been there since close to the beginning and learned to brew under Tim Yarrington, the original kettle master. "I believe in traditional styles, but I'll use all the latest technology and ingredients to effect that result," he explained. "I just started using a hopback I built to add more hop flavor and aroma to the Pale Ale and the Best Bitter." I can assure you it works beautifully! The Signature Pale Ale is tasting the best it ever has.

There are lots of big beers he'd like to brew as specialties, but the small system and limited num-

Beers brewed: Year-round: German Valley Amber, Long Valley Nut Brown (GABF Bronze, 2004; GABF Gold, 2005), Grist Mill Golden, Hookerman's Light Ale, Lazy Jake Porter (GABF Bronze, 1999; GABF Gold, 2000; GABF Gold, 2005), Long Valley Best Bitter (GABF Bronze, 2000). Seasonals: Signature Pale Ale, Joe's Oatmeal Stout, Stone Barn Stout, Alpha Dog Pale Ale.

ber of tanks preclude that. "My job is first and foremost to make money and keep the brewery profitable," he said. "With a 7-barrel system, I need to brew quite a bit just to keep up with demand. Brewing a barleywine or Imperial stout on a regular basis would tie up valuable tank space. I believe that making specialties does fulfill one's artistic bent, though, and adds fun to the process."

The brewpub now depends on the transient tourist trade for its livelihood, which is surprising for this secluded area. Most of the people get to the area only two or three times a year and stop in to enjoy the assortment of session beers that Joe and his assistant brew up. "I have a responsibility to my customers to brew a consistent menu of products," he said, and emphasized it: "Consistency is the key! They expect when they come here those two times that the beer they had before is going to be the same one they enjoyed last visit. I'm not looking to make over-the-top beers, just ones where you can drink two or three with dinner and still drive home safely."

They also look to be a family destination, where you can bring the wife and kids to enjoy a meal in a comfortable setting. You can choose from outdoor dining in the summer or fireplace dining in the winter.

Long Valley has entered its beers into the judging at the Great American Beer Festival in Denver since 1999. A GABF medal is a badge of honor for brewers nationwide, and this small brewery won first time out of the gate. The Lazy Jake Porter picked up a bronze medal that year and went on to win a gold the next and again in 2005. Several others have been awarded to the Best Bitter and Nut Brown in the last few events, bringing their total to six.

Joe finds that to be an affirmation of his brewing principles: keeping his beers tight to the styles and brewing them consistently every time, unusual in this age where so many look to make a name for themselves with odd ingredients and methods. Joe seems to think that can be a good thing for the industry, but it's not his style. "You can cover a lot of mistakes with hops and alcohol, but a good session beer has to be done right the first time. I can't afford to 'sewer' even one batch."

Recently, one of the outbuildings that was kept during the renovations was discovered to be a smokehouse. The chef now uses it to smoke meats and cheeses, and Joe plans on doing some malt for a smoked porter. Once again, traditional methods for traditional styles.

The Pick: Obviously, the Lazy Jake Porter is the Pick here. This multimedal award winner is a nice medium-bodied, roasty example of this English style, with lots of malt and a nice hop finish. The Best Bitter runs a very close second and makes a great cask-conditioned product.

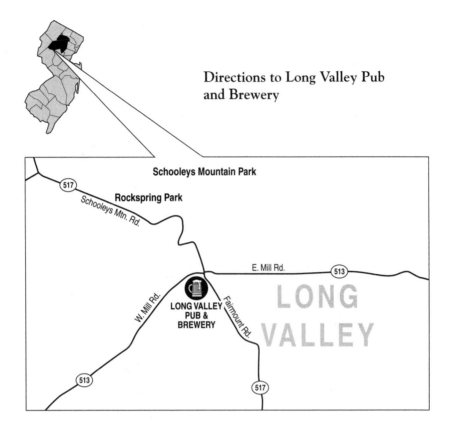

Directions to Long Valley Pub
and Brewery

Stop in and soak up some of the atmosphere as well as a few of those tasty session beers. Match them with a selection from the extensive culinary choices and make a day or night of it.

Opened: October 1995.
Owner: Long Valley Inc., LLC.
Brewer: Joe Saia.
System: 7-barrel Pub Brewing system, 750 barrels annual capacity.
Production: 735 barrels in 2006.
Brewpub hours: Monday through Wednesday, 11:30 A.M. to midnight; Thursday through Saturday, 11:30 A.M. to 2 A.M.; Sunday, noon to 10 P.M.
Tours: Upon special request.
Take-out beer: Half-gallon growlers.
Food: Bold American fare. A wide selection of appetizers, salads, substantial pub sandwiches, entrées, and desserts, featuring local foods where possible.

Extras: Full bar. Happy Hour weekdays 4 P.M. to 6:30 P.M.; $2.50 pints on Thursday. They carry some high-end whiskeys. (Yes, they do!— *Lew.*) Beer dinners in winter, based on seasonals. Music is provided when there are outdoor events.

Special considerations: Kids welcome. Vegetarian meals available. Handicapped-accessible.

Parking: Large lot on-site.

Lodging in the area: Neighbour House Bed and Breakfast, 143 West Mill Road, Long Valley, 908-876-3519; Comfort Inn Hackettstown, 1925 Route 52 West, Hackettstown, 908-813-8500.

Area attractions: The historic city of **Chester** is nearby, with a walking tour of the Old Village as well as some nice shopping and restaurants on Main Street. The **Obadiah La Tourette Grist and Saw Mill** (12 East Mill Road, Long Valley, 908-876-4478, www.wtlt.org/preserv_project_pg01.htm) is an interesting ongoing restoration of a large multipurpose water-powered mill. Tours are given most weekends, but visitors are warned that they may find themselves getting volunteered to do work on the restoration.

The work's already done at **Waterloo Village** (525 Waterloo Road, 973-347-0900, www.waterloovillage.org), open mid-April through mid-November. Here you'll find a re-creation of an inland port on the Morris Canal, a Lenni-Lenape Indian village, and craft shops. A multitude of craft fairs, festivals, and concerts are scheduled through the village's season.

Other area beer sites: There's just not a lot else out here. The only place within range is the **Laughing Lion** (40 North Sussex Street, Dover, 973-328-1800), and we didn't get a chance to visit it. I tried, but my directions had me half a mile away. It's supposed to have a good bottled beer selection, anyway. You may just have to satisfy yourself with Long Valley.

BEERWEBS

The Web has become a great place to share beer and bar information. But as with anything else on the Web, you have to use a little wisdom. Websites can be out of date, intensely subjective, poorly edited, and just plain wrong. Let the reader beware.

Here are the websites we use to find beers, bars, and beer geeks in the Mid-Atlantic region from New York to Virginia, and across the country. If we have any reservations about them, we've stated them.

www.lewbryson.com Lew's own website includes frequent online updates to this and his previous books: *New York Breweries; Virginia, Maryland, and Delaware Breweries;* and *Pennsylvania Breweries,* plus news on future guides in the series, links to some of his other writing, and other things he finds interesting.

www.pubcrawler.com Pubcrawler has slipped a bit, but it is still one of the two best brewery and bar locator sites. You can search more than six thousand North American breweries, brewpubs, and bars by name, city, state, zip code, or area code, and every entry has a map link for directions. The entries have phone numbers, addresses, links, logos, and most important, years of patron reviews. Our only reservations here are that some of the reviewers are obviously biased and that sometimes Pubcrawler's not as complete as it could be.

www.BeerAdvocate.com This is the other site we use for finding breweries and bars. BeerAdvocate is mostly about rating beers and talking about beers and talking about rating beers . . . but it is also an online community of people who really care about the beer they drink *and the beer you drink.* So the BeerAdvocate forums are a great place to get inside scoops on what's going on in bars. The website's online directory, BeerFly, has a wide range of listings for breweries, bars, and beer stores. Useful and entertaining site.

GLOSSARY

ABV/ABW. Alcohol by volume/alcohol by weight. These are two slightly different ways of measuring the alcohol content of beverages, as a percentage of either the beverage's total volume or its weight. For example, if you have 1 liter of 4 percent ABV beer, 4 percent of that liter (40 milliliters) is alcohol. However, because alcohol weighs only 79.6 percent as much as water, that same beer is only 3.18 percent ABW. This may seem like a dry exercise in mathematics, but it is at the heart of the common misconception that Canadian beer is stronger than American beer. Canadian brewers generally use ABV figures, whereas American brewers have historically used the lower ABW figures. Mainstream Canadian and American lagers are approximately equal in strength. Just to confuse the issue further, most American microbreweries use ABV figures. This is very important if you're trying to keep a handle on how much alcohol you're consuming. If you know how much Bud (at roughly 5 percent ABV) you can safely consume, you can extrapolate from there. Learn your limits . . . before you hit them.

Adjunct. Any nonbarley malt source of sugars for fermentation. This can be candy sugar, corn grits, corn or rice syrup, or one of any number of specialty grains. Wheat, rye, and candy sugars are considered by beer geeks to be "politically correct" adjuncts; corn and rice are generally taken as signs of swill. Small amounts of corn and rice, however, used as brewing ingredients for certain styles of beer, are slowly gaining acceptance in craft-brewing circles. Try to keep an open mind.

Ale. The generic term for warm-fermented beers.

Anheuser-Busch. Anheuser-Busch (A-B) is the world's second-largest brewer, with just under half of the U.S. market and about 8 percent of the world's market. Bud Light is the biggest-selling beer in the United States. Because of this, A-B is often the whipping boy of the microbrewers, but A-B has taken its share of shots at the micros as well. No one disputes the quality control and consistency of brewers like A-B. Lew has met Augie Busch; he is sharp, devoted to his company and its beers, and driven to improve the company's standing. A-B has more than a hundred highly trained and qualified brewmasters who are fanatical about quality in ingredients and process.

ATTTB. The federal Alcohol and Tobacco Tax and Trade Bureau, formerly part of the ATF, a branch of the Treasury Department. The ATTTB is the federal regulatory arm for the brewing industry. It has to inspect every brewery before it opens, approve every label before it is used, and approve all packaging. The ATTTB is also the body responsible for the fact that while every food, even bottled water, *must* have a nutritional information label, beer (and wine and cider and spirits) is *not allowed* to have one, even though it is a significant source of calories, carbohydrates, and in the case of unfiltered beers, B vitamins and protein. The problem is that sometimes every ATTTB agent and bureaucrat seems to have a different interpretation of the regulations, and sometimes they have a very negative attitude toward the beverages they're regulating. As a brewer once told me, "I'd enjoy this a lot more if [ATTTB] didn't make me feel like I was dealing in controlled substances."

Barley. A wonderfully apt grain for brewing beer. Barley grows well in relatively marginal soils and climates. It has no significant gluten content, which makes it unsuitable for baking bread and thereby limits market competition for brewers buying the grain. Its husk serves as a very efficient filter at the end of the mashing process. And it makes beer that tastes really, really good. Barley comes in two types: two-row and six-row, named for the rows of kernels on the heads of the grain. In days past, two-row barley was plumper and considered finer. Six-row barley was easier to grow, had a better yield per acre and higher enzymatic power, but had a somewhat astringent character. These differences have been lessened by cross-breeding. Most barley grown in North America is six-row, for reasons of soil and climate. (Incidentally, the grain's kernels, or corns, are the source of the name "John Barleycorn," a traditional personification of barley or beer.)

Barrel. A traditional measure of beer volume equal to 31 U.S. gallons. The most common containers of draft beer in the United States are half and quarter barrels, or kegs, at 15.5 gallons and 7.75 gallons, respectively, though the one-sixth-barrel kegs (about 5.2 gallons), known as sixtels, are becoming popular with microbrewers.

Beer. A fermented beverage brewed from grain, generally malted barley. "Beer" covers a variety of beverages, including ales and lagers, stouts and bocks, porters and pilsners, lambics and altbiers, cream ale, Kölsch, wheat beer, and a whole lot more.

Beer geek. A person who takes beer a little more seriously than does the average person. Lew has been chided for using the term *geek* here, but he hasn't found another one he likes, so our apologies to those who object. We call ourselves beer geeks, if that's any consolation. Often homebrewers, beer geeks love to argue with other beer geeks about what makes exceptional beers exceptional. That is, if they've been able to agree on which beers are exceptional in the first place. A beer geek is the kind of person who would buy a book about traveling to breweries . . . the kind of person who would read the glossary of a beer book. Hey, hi there!

Bottle-conditioned. A beer that has been bottled with an added dose of live yeast. This living yeast causes the beer to mature and change as it ages over periods of one to thirty years or more. It will also "eat" any oxygen that may have been sealed in at bottling and keep the beer from oxidizing, a staling process that leads to sherryish and "wet cardboard" aromas in beer. Bottle-conditioned beer qualifies as "real ale."

Brewer. One who brews beer for commercial sale.

Breweriana. Brewery and beer memorabilia, such as trays, coasters, neon signs, steins, mirrors, and so on, including the objects of desire of the beer can and bottle collectors. Most collectors do this for fun, a few do it for money (breweriana is starting to command some big prices; just check eBay), but the weird thing about this is the number of breweriana collectors—about a third, from our experience—who don't drink beer.

Brewhouse. The vessels used to mash the malt and grains and boil the wort. The malt and grains are mashed in a vessel called a *mash tun*. Brewhouse size is generally given in terms of the capacity of the brewkettle, where the wort is boiled. A brewery's annual capacity is a function of brewhouse size, fermentation and aging tank capacity, and the length of the aging cycle for the brewery's beers.

Brewpub. A brewery that sells the majority of its output on draft, on the premises, or a tavern that brews its own beer. New Jersey laws are particularly restrictive on brewpubs—it's very difficult to open more than one, and they can't bottle beer for off-premises sales—and craft breweries, where on-premises sales are limited to two six-packs per person.

CAMRA. The CAMpaign for Real Ale, a British beer drinkers' consumer group formed in the early 1970s by beer drinkers irate over the disappearance of cask-conditioned ale. They have been very vocal and successful in bringing this traditional drink back to a place of importance in the United Kingdom. CAMRA sets high standards for cask-conditioned ale, which only a few brewers in the United States match; the Ship Inn is one of them.

Carbonation. The fizzy effects of carbon dioxide (CO_2) in solution in a liquid such as beer. Carbonation can be accomplished artificially by injecting the beer with the gas or naturally by trapping the CO_2, which is a by-product of fermentation. There is no intrinsic qualitative difference between beers carbonated by these two methods. Brewer's choice, essentially. Low carbonation will allow a broader array of flavors to come through, whereas high carbonation can result in a perceived bitterness. Most American drinkers prefer a higher carbonation.

Cask. A keg designed to serve cask-conditioned ale by gravity feed or by handpump, not by gas pressure. These casks may be made of wood, but most are steel with special plumbing.

Cask-conditioned beer. An unfiltered beer that is put in a cask before it is completely ready to serve. The yeast still in the beer continues to work and ideally brings the beer to perfection at the point of sale, resulting in a beautifully fresh beer that has a "soft" natural carbonation and beautiful array of aromas. The flip side to achieving this supreme freshness is that as the beer is poured, air replaces it in the cask, and the beer will become sour within five days. Bars should sell the cask out before then or remove it from sale. If you are served sour cask-conditioned beer, send it back. Better yet, ask politely for a taste before ordering. Cask-conditioned beer is generally served at cellar temperature (55 to 60 degrees Fahrenheit) and is lightly carbonated. Cask-conditioned beers are almost always ales, but some American brewers are experimenting with cask-conditioned lager beers. The Ship Inn will sell you cask-conditioned beer in their beer-in-a-box package, a common package for cask ale in the United Kingdom, where it's known as a *polypin*.

Cold-filtering. The practice of passing finished beer through progressively finer filters (usually cellulose or ceramic) to strip out microorganisms that can spoil the beer when it is stored. Brewers like Coors and Miller, and also some smaller brewers, use cold-filtering as an alternative to pasteurization (see below). Some beer geeks complain that this "strip-filtering" robs beers of their more subtle complexities and some of their body. We're not sure about that, but we do know that unfiltered beer right from the brewery tank almost always tastes more intense than the filtered, packaged beer.

Contract brewer. A brewer who hires an existing brewery to brew beer on contract. Contract brewers range from those who simply have a different label put on one of the brewery's existing brands to those who maintain a separate on-site staff to actually brew the beer at the brewery. Some brewers and beer geeks feel contract-brewed beer is inherently inferior. This is strictly a moral and business issue; some of the best beers on the market are contract-brewed.

Craft brewer. The new term for *microbrewer*. Craft brewer, like microbrewer before it, is really a code word for any brewer producing beers other than mainstream American lagers like Budweiser. (See "A word about . . . Micros, Brewpubs, and Craft Brewers" on page 50.)

Decoction. The type of mashing often used by lager brewers to wring the full character from the malt. In a decoction mash, a portion of the hot mash is taken to another vessel, brought to boiling, and returned to the mash, thus raising the temperature. See also *infusion*.

Draft. Beer dispensed from a tap, whether from a keg or cask. Draft beer is not pasteurized, is kept under optimum conditions throughout the wholesaler-retailer chain, and is shockingly cheaper than bottled or canned beer (each half-barrel keg is more than seven cases of beer; check some prices and do the math). Kegs are available in 5-, 7.75-, and 15.5-gallon sizes, and almost all are now the straight-sided kegs with handles. New Jersey doesn't have an ineffective and intrusive keg registration law—at least, not yet. Kegs are also ultimately recyclable, with a lifespan of forty *years*. Do what we do: Get draft beer for your next party.

Dry-hopping. Adding hops to the beer in postfermentation stages, often in porous bags to allow easy removal. This results in a greater hop aroma in the finished beer. A few brewers put a small bag of hop cones in each cask of their cask-conditioned beers, resulting in a particularly intense hop aroma in a glass of the draft beer.

ESB. Extra Special Bitter, an ale style with a rich malt character and full body, perhaps some butter or butterscotch aromas, and an understated hop bitterness. An ESB is noticeably bitter only in comparison with a mild ale, a style not often found in America.

Esters. Aroma compounds produced by fermentation that gives some ales lightly fruity aromas: banana, pear, and grapefruit, among others. The aromas produced are tightly linked to the yeast strain used. Ester-based aromas should not be confused with the less subtle fruit aromas of a beer to which fruit or fruit essences have been added.

Extract. More specifically, malt extract. Malt extract is kind of like concentrated wort (see below). Malt is mashed and the resulting sweet, unhopped wort is reduced to a syrup. This is important to know because some breweries brew with malt extract. In extract brewing, the extract is mixed with water and boiled. Specialty grains (such as black patent or chocolate malt, wheat, or roasted barley) can be added for flavor notes and nuances. It is actually more expensive to brew with extract, but you need less equipment, which can be crucial in cramped brewing areas. The quality of the beer may suffer as well. Some people claim to be able to pick out extract brews. We've had extract brews that had a common taste—a kind of thin, vegetal sharpness—but we've also had excellent extract brews at various breweries. Our advice is to try it yourself.

Fermentation. The miracle of yeast; the heart of making beer. Fermentation is the process in which yeast turns sugar and water into alcohol, heat, carbon dioxide, esters, and traces of other compounds.

Final gravity. See *gravity*.

Firkin. A cask or keg holding 9 gallons of beer, specially plumbed for gravity or handpump dispense.

Geekerie. The collective of beer geeks, particularly the beer-oriented, beer-fascinated, beer-above-all beer geeks. The geekerie sometimes can fall victim to group thinking and a herd mentality, but they are generally good people, if a bit hopheaded and malt-maniacal. If you're not a member of the geekerie, you might want to consider getting to know them: They usually know where all the best bars and beer stores are in their town, and they're more than happy to share the knowledge and even go along with you to share the fun. All you have to do is ask. See the Beerwebs section for links to the better beer pages, a good way to hook up with them.

Gravity. The specific gravity of wort (original gravity) or finished beer (terminal gravity). The ratio of dissolved sugars to water determines the gravity of the wort. If there are more dissolved sugars, the original gravity and the potential alcohol are higher. The sugar that is converted to alcohol by the yeast lowers the terminal gravity and makes the beer drier, just like wine. A brewer can determine the alcohol content of a beer by mathematical comparison of its original gravity and terminal gravity.

Great American Beer Festival (GABF). Since 1982, America's breweries have been invited each year to bring their best beer to the GABF in Denver to showcase what America can brew. Since 1987, the GABF has awarded medals for various styles of beer; seventy-five styles were judged in 2007, three medals for each style. To ensure impartiality, the beers are tasted blind, their identities hidden from the judges. GABF medals are the most prestigious awards in American brewing because of the festival's longevity and reputation for fairness.

Growler. A jug or bottle used to take home draft beer. These are usually either simple half-gallon glass jugs with screwtops or more elaborate molded glass containers with swingtop seals. Lew has traced the origin of the term *growler* back to a cheap, four-wheeled horse cab in use in Victorian London. These cabs would travel a circuit of pubs in the evenings, and riding from pub to pub was known as "working the growler." To bring a pail of beer home to have with dinner was to anticipate the night's work of drinking and became known as "rushing the growler." When the growler cabs disappeared from the scene, we were left with only the phrase, and "rushing the growler" was assumed to mean hurrying home with the bucket. When Ed Otto revived the practice by selling jugs of Otto Brothers beer at his Jackson Hole brewery in the mid-1980s, he called them growlers. Now you know where the term really came from.

Guest taps/guest beers. Beers made by other brewers that are offered at brewpubs.

Handpump. A hand-powered pump for dispensing beer from a keg, also called a *beer engine*. Either a handpump or a gravity tap (putting the barrel on the bar and pounding in a simple spigot) is always used for dispensing cask-conditioned beer; however, the presence of a handpump does not guarantee that the beer being dispensed is cask-conditioned.

Homebrewing. Making honest-to-goodness beer at home for personal consumption. Homebrewing is where many American craft brewers got their start.

Hops. The spice of beer. Hop plants (*Humulus lupus*) are vines whose flowers have a remarkable effect on beer. The flowers' resins and oils add bitterness and a variety of aromas (spicy, piney, citrusy, and others) to the finished beer. Beer without hops would be more like a fizzy, sweet "alco-soda."

IBU. International Bittering Unit, a measure of a beer's bitterness. Humans can first perceive bitterness at levels between 8 and 12 IBU. Budweiser has 11.5 IBU, Heineken 18, Sierra Nevada Pale Ale 32, Pilsner Urquell 43, and a monster like Sierra Nevada Bigfoot clocks in at 98 IBU. Equivalent amounts of bitterness will seem greater in a lighter-bodied beer, whereas a heavier, maltier beer like Bigfoot needs lots of bitterness to be perceived as balanced.

Imperial. A beer style intensifier, indicating a beer that is hoppier and stronger. Once there was an Imperial court in St. Petersburg, Russia, the court of the czars. It supported a trade with England in strong, heavy, black beers, massive versions of the popular English porters, which became known as imperial porters and somewhat later as imperial stouts. Then in the late 1990s, American brewers started brewing IPAs with even more hops than the ridiculous amounts they were already using, at a gravity that led to beers of 7.5 percent ABV and up. What to call them? They looked at the imperial stouts and grabbed the apparent intensifier: "Imperial" IPA was born. While this is still the most common usage, this shorthand for "hoppier and stronger" has been applied to pilsner and, amusingly, porter. Where it will stop, no one knows, as brewers joke about brewing "imperial mild" and "imperial helles." There is a move toward using "double" instead of "imperial."

Infusion. The mashing method generally used by ale brewers. Infusion entails heating the mash in a single vessel until the starches have been converted to sugar. There is single infusion, in which the crushed malt (grist) is mixed with hot water and steeped without further heating, and step infusion, in which the mash is held for short periods at rising temperature points. Infusion mashing is simpler than decoction mashing and works well with most types of modern malt.

IPA. India Pale Ale, a British ale style that has been almost completely co-opted by American brewers, characterized in this country by intense hops bitterness, accompanied in better examples of the style by a full-malt body. The name derives from the style's origin as a beer brewed for export to British beer drinkers in India. The beer was strong and heavily laced with hops—a natural preservative—to better endure the long sea voyage. Some British brewers claim that the beer was brewed that way in order to be diluted upon arrival in India, a kind of "beer concentrate" that saved on shipping costs.

Kräusening. The practice of carbonating beer by a second fermentation. After the main fermentation has taken place and its vigorous blowoff of carbon dioxide has been allowed to escape, a small amount of fresh wort is added to the tank. A second fermentation takes place, and the carbon dioxide is captured in solution. General opinion is that there is little sensory difference between kräusened beer and beer carbonated by injection, but some brewers use this more traditional method.

Lager. The generic term for all cold-fermented beers. Lager has also been appropriated as a name for the lightly hopped pilsners that have become the world's most popular beers, such as Budweiser, Ki-Rin, Brahma, Heineken, and Foster's. Many people speak of pilsners and lagers as if they are two different syles of beer, which is incorrect. All pilsners are lagers, but not all lagers are pilsners. Some are bocks, hellesbiers, and Märzens.

Lambic. A very odd style of beer brewed in Belgium that could take pages to explain. Suffice it to say that the beer is fermented spontaneously by airborne wild yeasts and bacteria that are resident in the aged wooden fermenting casks. The beer's sensory characteristics have been described as funky, barnyard, and horseblanket . . . it's an acquired taste. But once you have that taste, lambics can be extremely rewarding. Most knowledgeable people believe that the beers can be brewed only in a small area of Belgium, because of the peculiarities of the wild yeasts. But some American brewers have had a degree of success in replicating this character by carefully using prepared cultures of yeasts and bacteria.

Malt. Generally this refers to malted barley, although other grains can be malted and used in brewing. Barley is wetted and allowed to sprout, which causes the hard, stable starches in the grain to convert to soluble starches (and small amounts of sugars). The grains, now called malt, are kiln-dried to kill the sprouts and conserve the starches. Malt is responsible for the color of beer. The kilned malt can be roasted like a French roast coffee, which will darken its color and intensify its flavors.

Mash. A mixture of cracked grains of malt and water, which is then heated. Heating causes starches in the malt to convert to sugars, which will be consumed by the yeast in fermentation. The length of time the mash is heated, temperatures, and techniques used are crucial to the character of the finished beer. Two mashing techniques are infusion and decoction.

Megabrewer. A mainstream brewer, generally producing 5 million or more barrels of American-style pilsner beer annually. Anheuser-Busch, Miller, and Coors are the best-known megabrewers.

Microbrewer. A somewhat dated term, originally defined as a brewer producing less than 15,000 barrels of beer in a year. Microbrewer, like craft brewer, is generally applied to any brewer producing beers other than mainstream American lagers. (See "A word about . . . Micros, Brewpubs, and Craft Brewers" on page 50.)

Original gravity. See *gravity*.

Pasteurization. A process named for its inventor, Louis Pasteur, the famed French microbiologist. Pasteurization involves heating beer to kill the microorganisms in it. This keeps beer fresh longer, but unfortunately it also changes the flavor, because the beer is essentially cooked. "Flash pasteurization" sends fresh beer through a heated pipe where most of the microorganisms are killed; here the beer is hot for only twenty seconds or so, as opposed to the twenty to thirty minutes of regular "tunnel" pasteurization. See also *cold-filtering*.

Pilsner. The Beer That Conquered the World. Developed in 1842 in Pilsen (now Plzen, in the Czech Republic), it is a hoppy pale lager that quickly became known as *pilsner* or *pilsener*, a German word meaning simply "from Pilsen." Pilsner rapidly became the most popular beer in the world and now accounts for more than 80 percent of all beer consumed worldwide. A less hoppy, more delicate version of pilsner called *budweiser* was developed in the Czech town of Budejovice, formerly known as Budweis. Anheuser-Busch's Budweiser, the world's best-selling beer, is quite a different animal.

Pitching. The technical term for adding yeast to wort.

Prohibition. The period from 1920 to 1933 when the sale, manufacture, or transportation of alcoholic beverages was illegal in the United States, thanks to the Eighteenth Amendment and the Volstead Act. Prohibition had a disastrous effect on American brewing and brought about a huge growth in organized crime and government corruption. Repeal of Prohibition came with ratification of the Twenty-first Amendment in December 1933. Beer drinkers, however, had gotten an eight-month head start when the Volstead Act, the enforcement legislation of Prohibition, was amended to allow sales of 3.2 percent ABW beer. The amendment took effect at midnight, April 7. According to Will Anderson's *From Beer to Eternity,* more than 1 million barrels of beer were consumed on April 7: 2,323,000 six-packs each hour.

Quaff and quaffability. Quaff means to drink large quantities. With craft brews, this usually means a pint or more. A pale ale generally is quaffable; a doublebock generally is not. A good, truly quaffable doublebock would be dangerous, given the style's usual alcohol levels!

Real ale. See *cask-conditioned beer.*

Regional brewery. Somewhere between a micro- and a megabrewer. Annual production by regional breweries ranges from 35,000 to 2 million barrels. They generally brew mainstream American lagers. However, some microbrewers—Boston Beer Company, New Belgium, and Sierra Nevada, for instance—have climbed to this production level, and some regional brewers, such as Anchor, Matt's, and August Schell, have reinvented themselves and now produce craft-brewed beer. (See "A word about . . . Micros, Brewpubs, and Craft Brewers" on page 50.)

Reinheitsgebot. The German beer purity law, which has its roots in a 1516 Bavarian statute limiting the ingredients in beer to barley malt, hops, and water. The law evolved into an inch-thick book and was the cornerstone of high-quality German brewing. It was deemed anticompetitive by the European Community courts and overturned in 1988. Most German brewers, however, continue to brew by its standards; tradition and the demands of their customers ensure it.

Repeal. See *Prohibition.*

Ringwood yeast. The house yeast of Peter Austin and Pugsley System breweries. A very particular yeast that requires an open fermenter, it is mostly found on the East Coast. Some well-known examples of Ringwood-brewed beers are Geary's, Magic Hat, and Shipyard; the Ship Inn has a classic Peter Austin brewing system. Ringwood beers are often easily identifiable by a certain nuttiness to their flavor. A brewer who isn't careful will find that Ringwood has created an undesirably high level of diacetyl, a compound that gives a beer a buttery or butterscotch aroma. Note that smaller amounts of diacetyl are perfectly normal and desirable in some types of beer.

Session beer. A beer that is low to medium-low in strength, say 3 to 4.2 percent ABV, but still flavorful, designed for what the British call "session drinking," the kind that goes on all afternoon through tons of talk and maybe some snacks, and doesn't leave you knee-wobbling after 4 pints.

Sixtel. A new size of keg developed in 1996, holding one-sixth of a barrel: 5.2 gallons, or about two and a half cases. Very popular for home use (well, we love 'em!), and popular with multitaps as well. The beer stays fresher, and you can fit more different beers in a cold box. The word *sixtel* is of uncertain origin; it was not coined by the developer of the keg but apparently grew up among the users.

Swill. A derogatory term used by beer geeks for American mainstream beers. The beers do not really deserve the name, since they are made with pure ingredients under conditions of quality control and sanitation some micros only wish they could achieve.

Terminal gravity. See *gravity*.

Three-tier system. A holdover from before Prohibition, the three-tier system requires brewers, wholesalers, and retailers to be separate entities. The system was put in place to curtail financial abuses that were common when the three were mingled. Owning both wholesale and retail outlets gave unscrupulous brewers the power to rake off huge amounts of money, which all too often was used to finance political graft and police corruption. The three-tier system keeps the wholesaler insulated from pressure from the brewer and puts a layer of separation between brewer and retailer. Recent court rulings have put the future of the regulated three-tier system in serious doubt, which may spell paradise or disaster for beer drinkers.

Wort. The prebeer grain broth of sugars, proteins, hop oils, alpha acids, and whatever else was added or developed during the mashing process. Once the yeast has been pitched and starts its jolly work, wort becomes beer.

Yeast. A miraculous fungus that, among other things, converts sugar into alcohol and carbon dioxide. The particular yeast strain used in brewing beer greatly influences the aroma and flavor of the beer. An Anheuser-Busch brewmaster once told Lew that the yeast strain used there is the major factor in the flavor and aroma of Budweiser. Yeast is the sole source of the clovey, banana-rama aroma and the taste of Bavarian-style wheat beers. The original Reinheitsgebot of 1516 made no mention of yeast; it hadn't been discovered yet. Early brewing depended on a variety of sources for yeast: adding a starter from the previous batch of beer; exposing the wort to the wild yeasts carried on the open air (a method still used for Belgian lambic beers); always using the same vats for fermentation (yeast would cling to cracks and pores in the wood); or stirring the beer with a "magic stick" (which had the dormant yeast from the last batch dried on its surface). British brewers called the turbulent, billowing foam on fermenting beer *goddesgood*—"God is good"— because the foam meant that the predictable magic of the yeast was making beer. Amen.

Zwickel. A *zwickel* ("tzVICK-el") is a little spout coming off the side of a beer tank that allows the brewer to sample the maturing beer in small amounts; it is also sometimes called a *pigtail*. If you're lucky, your tour will include an unfiltered sample of beer tapped directly from the tank through this little spout. Some brewers are touchy about this, as the zwickel is a potential site for infection, but with proper care, it's perfectly harmless to "tickle the zwickel." It's delicious, too: Unfiltered beer is the hot ticket.

INDEX

Also by Lew Bryson . . .

PENNSYLVANIA
BREWERIES

3RD EDITION

by Lew Bryson

978-0-8117-3222-2

A guide to the state's 53 regional breweries,
microbreweries, and brewpubs.

WWW.STACKPOLEBOOKS.COM
1-800-732-3669

Also in the Breweries series . . .

NEW YORK BREWERIES
by Lew Bryson
978-0-8117-2817-1

MICHIGAN BREWERIES
by Paul Ruschmann
& Maryanne Nasiatka
978-0-8117-3299-4

VIRGINIA, MARYLAND,
& DELAWARE BREWERIES
by Lew Bryson
978-0-8117-3215-4

WWW.STACKPOLEBOOKS.COM
1-800-732-3669